PRAISE FOR
CREATING THE IMPOSSIBLE

Creating the Impossible *is a must-read for anyone who has a dream. With step-by-step principles woven within amazing stories of dreams getting fulfilled, this book will allow you to take your journey into the unknown where your dreams become real.*

~ Chris Attwood, co-author of the NY Times bestsellers *The Passion Test* and *Your Hidden Riches*, and founder and CEO of Beyul Club & Resorts.

This is a book about courage and possibility. We all can benefit from knowing what it takes to move our visions from our imaginations to our reality. With real-life examples from transformational leaders, including Barbara Edie's own inspiring stories, Creating the Impossible *shows us how.*

~ Teresa de Grosbois, #1 International best-selling author of *Mass Influence*, international speaker and founder of the Evolutionary Business Council.

If you've had an inkling you're meant to do something bigger, perhaps even seemingly impossible, this beautiful book illuminates the path to follow that inner knowing and bring your vision to life. It fills your heart and boosts your confidence to manifest even those "impossible" dreams.

~ Ellen Rogin, co-author of the New York Times bestseller *Picture Your Prosperity*.

Absolutely engaging and inspiring...I read the book in one sitting! With compelling stories, powerful lessons, and questions for contemplation woven throughout, Creating the Impossible *shows us time after time when we trust our inner wisdom, dream big, and follow our hearts, anything is possible!*

~ Pamela Thompson, #1 Best-selling author of *Learning to Dance with Life: A Guide for High Achieving Women*, and President and CEO, Creative Life Coaching Inc. and founder of the Creative Living Community.

"If you are the bearer of a dream, it is likely yours to deliver to the world" and Barbara Edie has done just that. *She listened to her heart. This book demonstrates it is not about having all the answers or at times even knowing the how, it's about listening to your inner calling. An enduring and meaningful piece that will stir you!*

~ Jo Dibblee, Frock Off Inc., Breakthrough expert, author, and event producer.

A life-altering, soul-shaking book ... and powerful guide to manifesting what YOUR heart truly wants. It's changed the way I live—and create—my life.

~ Mischelle Van Thiel, CEO of Victoria Hospice, entrepreneur, and business & lifestyle coach

As someone who has healed from "incurable" cancer, I know that you can create the impossible. Barbara Edie's beautifully authentic voice and powerful stories guide you on the steps to make those 'impossible' dreams happen. A gem of a book.

~ Annie Pool, International best-selling author of the upcoming book *Passport to Life: How I Overcame Incurable Cancer Through the Power of Travel.*

BARBARA EDIE

CREATING
THE IMPOSSIBLE
WHAT IT TAKES TO BRING YOUR VISION TO LIFE

Livonia, Michigan

Also by Barbara Edie:
*Sparking Change Around the Globe: 5 Ways to
Make Your Difference in the World*

Cover design, interior book design,
and eBook design by Blue Harvest Creative
www.blueharvestcreative.com

Creating the Impossible: What It Takes to Bring Your Vision to Life

Published by Zander
an imprint of BHC Press

Library of Congress Control Number:
2016957830

ISBN-13: 978-1-946006-19-6
ISBN-10: 1-946006-19-X

Visit the author at:
www.barbaraedie.com &
www.bhcpress.com

Also available in eBook

This book is dedicated to my mom, *Lois Edie*, who instilled in me at a young age the idea, "To thine own self be true"—regardless of the opinions, beliefs, or thoughts of others, including those who say it is "impossible." She also taught me to never, ever, give up. Thanks, Mom, for always inspiring me to follow my heart and true nature—no matter what—to create my own (sometimes amazing) reality.

CONTENTS

FOREWORD
BY MARCI SHIMOFF

Can you achieve the impossible and have your biggest vision become a reality?

That's a question I have frequently pondered, and one I imagine you probably have, too. In a world where many people are struggling just to get through the day, there's often a paralyzing belief that we're simply too small or powerless to bring what we truly desire into our lives or help create a world we want to live in.

Then along comes a book like *Creating the "Impossible,"* which not only offers the perfect antidote to any sense of hopelessness but also outlines the bold steps you can take to follow your heart and bring your vision into reality. A book where story after story demonstrates the magnitude of what one person—anyone—with focus, vision, and inspired action can create and the impact he or she can have on the world. If you've ever wondered how one person can achieve what others might call miracles, you'll meet many people here who are doing precisely that. And they're not just transforming their own lives; they're creating projects, programs, and organizations that are having a significant effect on both individuals and society.

In the past 20 years, I've had the honor to be a #1 *New York Times* best-selling author many times over; I was featured in the book and hit film *The Secret*, and I have spoken to audiences of thousands around the world. So I understand what it takes to bring big visions to life, and I've helped many others do this very thing. In my courses and trainings, I've mentored thousands of people to create what they once thought was impossible and to lead what I call a miraculous life. I don't believe miracles are possible—I know they are.

Also, in research for my book *Happy for No Reason*, I discovered that deeply happy people make it a priority to contribute to something greater than themselves. Many people who are "happy for no reason" are realizing big visions, living their dreams, and passionately engaging in meaningful service to a larger cause.

My colleague and best-selling author Barbara Edie has a desire to serve and contribute to something greater than herself. When I first met Barbara in an author-mentoring program I led, I could see she was a person of profound caring and compassion. She has a deep and authentic desire to empower people to create a better world—for others as well as for themselves.

A former acute-care nurse and trained journalist, she has a nurse's empathy, a writer's curiosity and talent for storytelling, and a humanitarian's heart. This powerful combination of kindness, passion, skill, and experience makes her the perfect person to write this book. A self-described global soul, Barbara has also traveled, studied, and lived on three continents, manifesting many of her own dreams while witnessing the inspiring efforts of others to transform lives . . . in some of the most desperate parts of the planet.

We've all heard the well-known advice, "Be the change you wish to see in the world." Well, like the leaders featured in this book, Barbara hopes to foster social change by presenting a fresh approach to building a better world. Instead of focusing on eliminating "what's wrong," we turn our energy to *creating* the results we want to bring forth. We commit to what's *possible*, not just probable.

In one of our author workshops, I remember interviewing Barbara about her book, and she said, "You don't have to go global to be noble." It was a memorable moment, as it captured an important part of Barbara's message: that even small visions—in your local community or on your own front porch—can create great change. You'll see that in this book. Barbara captures the compelling and amazing stories of real-life visionaries and powerful creators who have answered their soul's calling and mastered certain principles that have allowed them to expand their vision and live their dream.

You, too, can apply these principles to create a more meaningful, fulfilling life. In my research, I've discovered that authentically happy people see the whole world as their family. Their love, compassion, and caring extend beyond relatives and friends to all of humankind. Happy people make it a habit to give whatever they can, wherever they can.

In the bigger picture, doing what you love and serving others brings more than just personal happiness to you—it's critical to having peace, happiness, and prosperity on this planet. When we create a life we love *and* it benefits others, we create greater peace in our hearts, which helps create more peace in the world. As the Hopi prayer quoted in Barbara's introduction says so poignantly, "We are the ones we've been waiting for."

I believe that each of us is here on the planet with a purpose, a specific way in which we can best offer our gifts to the world. Through the stories in this inspiring new book, you'll learn that you and I can manifest our dreams—big and small—and make the difference we came here to make.

INTRODUCTION
BY BARBARA EDIE

This book demonstrates the power of anyone with a steadfast vision to bring forth what he or she wants to create, no matter how "impossible" others might say it is. We've all had dreams we never imagined would come true—until they did. What some call miracles, others call reality.

Here you'll find stories, including my own, of men and women who have discovered the secrets and techniques not only to create what they love and to see their great vision come to fruition but also, in some cases, to create what others said would never happen.

More specifically, while some people dream of fame and fortune, winning an Oscar or Grammy, founding their own company, or running for office—all worthy aspirations—I chose to focus on people whose vision had an altruistic or humanitarian component, a dream that when realized would impact lives and "do a world of good" by doing good in the world.

A Search for Meaning

The idea for this book started when I was searching for my own truth: What did I really come to the planet to do? What did I want to create in life, beyond my wildest dreams, before my time was up? And what was my vision? I *needed* a vision.

At the time, my "get up and go" had gotten up and left; my enthusiasm for work, my passion for life, and my "why" had left the building. I was in a lull in my career, making my living as a writer in a way that was enjoyable but not deeply fulfilling. I was writing—and living—from a safe place, not out on a limb, where the best fruit—the richness of life—awaits. I lived in a beautiful home, close to the water, with a front yard that looked like a small park. My health was good. My friends and family were happy and healthy. Everything was "fine" . . . and yet I felt empty, directionless, as if I was living an inauthentic life, hiding under a cloak of invisibility.

Have you ever felt that way? That life is rolling along just fine, but you haven't even come close to tapping into your greatness, to creating those dreams that are still keeping you up at night or realizing those goals that are still on your vision board? I had a deep longing for more—not more money, love, exotic vacations, or even shoes—but more *meaning* in my life.

To lift me out of my funk, a good friend invited me to watch a short film by *National Geographic* photographer Dewitt Jones, titled *Celebrating What's Right with the World.* Jones discovered an approach to his photography that changed not only his pictures but also his life's vision. On every assignment, whether photographing a field of dandelions, the Highland Games, or the world's finest weaver, he would look for the best in that moment and, in doing so, discover extraordinary images, people, and stories. He found that by focusing on and celebrating what was right with the world, he built a vision of possibility, not scarcity. It became his life philosophy and the basis of his work.

That was it! I asked myself, *What is my vision of possibility?* I found the answer on another continent. Actually, on a couple of other continents, on two different life-changing trips—to India and Africa—both of which I talk about later in this book.

In interviewing several leaders of transformation for this book and other projects, I discovered that creating your vision starts with a simple choice. Visionary artist Vanessa German countered violence in her inner-city neighborhood by teaching art (and kindness) to at-risk kids on her front porch; Canadian professor Bathélemy Bolivar created an online education program for high school students in his homeland of Haiti when children lost their schools and some of their teachers in a devastating earthquake; and Valentino Giacomin changed the face of education in India beginning with just three schools, very little money, and a lot of meditation. Then there's real-life rocket scientist Shubham Garg, who, in literally shooting for the stars, focused his efforts on giving everyday people the opportunity to launch into orbit and see Earth from space. These are just a few examples of what is possible when vision joins forces with focused, inspired action.

The principles discussed in this book and illustrated in the accompanying stories follow the arc of the classic hero's journey: answering the call to leave the ordinary world; surmounting obstacles; finding wisdom (like gold that has been transformed from lead); and bringing the gold, or wisdom, home—that is, manifesting the vision. As part of my own soul's journey to understand what it takes to bring one's vision to life, I interviewed and gathered stories from leaders who were creating extraordinary change. I found them to be awakened, dedicated, powerful beyond measure, and, most of all, *real*. Represented here are teachers, executives, mothers, artists, doctors, entrepreneurs, a yoga instructor, and an astronautical engineer. And while they all share common practices of success, each chapter features leaders whose stories best exemplify a particular principle or step on the journey of turning one's vision into reality. My own stories are included, too.

A Place to Begin

For those with grand visions, creating significant change can take a long time. It may not happen in one's lifetime, but even that seemingly daunting fact is an opportunity for spiritual growth. Bob Roth, renowned meditation teacher and executive director of the David Lynch Foundation, once shared with me our primary mission as human beings: "Established in being, take action." When you connect with the place of silence within you, and then act in the material world and persist in going for your vision, it can become a reality—but it all starts with who you are *being*.

Every powerful creator had to start somewhere—usually small, usually locally. Mother Teresa once noted that she had picked up 42,000 people from the streets of Calcutta—but she had started with one. She pointed out, "If I hadn't picked up that one, I would never have picked up the 42,000 others."

Sometimes creating your vision requires being shaken out of complacency and taking a long, honest look at where you are focusing your time and efforts. Neale Donald Walsch, author of the *Conversations with God* book series, said: "Ninety-eight percent of people in the world are spending ninety-eight percent of their time on things that don't matter."

Let's face it, parts of the world are troubled, and parts of our own lives are a big, hot mess. However, focusing on fixing problems isn't solving them; we're simply mitigating the chaos and pain until the problem returns.

"Problem solving is taking action to have something go away— the problem. Creating is taking action to have something come into being—the creation," says Robert Fritz, author of *The Path of Least Resistance*. If you eliminate the problem, the problem is now absent. Yet you still haven't created a result you actually want. At best, problem solving can bring temporary relief from a specific situation, but it seldom leads to final success.

So what *will* bring forth success—both personal and global? I suggest a very different approach. If we consciously choose to focus on *creating* the results we envision, rather than *avoiding* the reality that exists, new results will show up, both in our own personal world and the physical world around us. "When people are united with their real power—the power to create what they want to create— they always choose what is highest in humanity," says Fritz.

Your vision may not involve "changing the world," and that's just fine, but to manifest any vision, big or small, compelling results depend on the level of consciousness and the orientation—soul-driven or ego-driven—you are coming from.

Today, many people believe that as individuals we don't have the power to create the results we *truly* want—because we see them as extraordinary and impossible. Yet by limiting ourselves to only what we perceive as possible or reasonable, the best we can do is compromise—and this is not true success. This book offers an antidote to that limited vision and sense of powerlessness, which simply stems from not knowing the secrets, structure, and techniques to becoming a powerful creative force—in your own life or that of others. The stories that follow, including my own, demonstrate the magnitude of what *anyone* with the right vision, focus, and action can bring into reality.

Last, while many of the people featured here are powerful creators and have achieved phenomenal results, they are human beings just like you and me. That said, they have *applied* certain principles and practices, which you can, too, to become a creative force and achieve levels of success that others might call impossible.

That is my deepest wish (and vision) for all of us—to succeed at what matters most to us, and to create lives we love and a world we all want to live in.

In the words of a Hopi prayer: "We are the ones we've been waiting for."

"People who say it cannot be done should not inter-
rupt those who are doing it."

~ Aphorism ~

TRUTH
ANSWERING THE CALL

*"We must be willing to get rid of the life we've planned,
so as to have the life that is waiting for us."*

~ Joseph Campbell ~

I've had my share of wake-up calls—a suicidal depression, *four* near-fatal motor vehicle accidents, a 6.8-magnitude earthquake, and a near-drowning, to name just a few. Given these multiple brushes with death and frequent less-than-friendly reminders of life's finality, you'd think I would have answered my soul's calling a lot sooner. It's not that I haven't followed, and realized, many dreams; I have. However, lately, they seem to be getting bigger, and more urgent. My dreams are repetitive, and persistent; they're keeping me up at night.

In her book *Big Magic*, Elizabeth Gilbert says she believes ideas seek human collaborators and "that ideas *do* have a conscious will...that ideas *will* always try to seek the swiftest and most efficient conduit to the earth (just as lightning does)." I feel the same way about dreams, or what you might call your soul's truth. Your dreams come to you for a reason; they are seeking a soul willing to collaborate, and their selection process is far from random. If you are the bearer of a dream, it is likely yours to deliver to the world— if you so choose.

Having had a loved one die suddenly, inches from my side, I am perhaps more acutely aware than others that we have only so many days on this planet, and following our truth in order to create something meaningful seems like a good way to spend that time. So when my soul calls, I like to pick up its messages.

One of those recent messages led to an inspired decision to follow my heart and travel to Africa for a few weeks of wild, soul-inspired writer's training with William Whitecloud, author of *The Magician's Way* and *The Last Shaman*.

William and I first met virtually, on a Skype call, when the founder of the Evolutionary Business Council, a group to which we both belong, suggested we meet. In discussing our shared loved of writing, William told me about his training in high-level creativity and about an upcoming writer's workshop he was leading—in Africa. I had intended to go to Africa four years before, but I didn't get there and had put that dream on the shelf. Now, the opportunity to combine my love of writing and adventure with the energy and spirit of Africa was so compelling I could literally feel it in my cells. Before the call ended, I'd made the decision to cancel a planned trip to Peru and sign on to show up in Swaziland, in southern Africa, and "meet my writer's genius" in a transformational course. In a few short weeks, I would travel to the other side of the world to a country I had to look up on a map, to be with people I'd never met, in a program I knew nothing about, guided by an author whose books I had never read.

Crazy, you say? Following one's truth can seem that way. I've spent much of my life in the space of the unknown, and my soul has almost come to expect traveling without a map. I knew this trip to

Africa was a date with destiny—my destiny—and I really didn't need to know anything else.

Your heart wants what it wants. No logic is required; no explanations are needed. When you've been called to do something extraordinary, and you "follow your bliss," as Joseph Campbell said, "doors will open where you didn't know they were going to be."

During the training in Africa, we did a meditation called "Land of Plenty," to connect with our inner guidance and truth about what, in our Land of Plenty, where we could have *anything*, we were really here to create. When I checked in with my guides, they had big plans for me. Part of this was writing a book about what it really takes to lead a soul-inspired life and bring one's visions to reality. In the meditation, I also had a vision of teaching others about the principles of manifesting what they love—and providing this training in . . . where else but Africa!

And speaking of doors swinging open unexpectedly, at the time of this writing, I returned to Africa, specifically for a "soul safari" and more deep work with William Whitecloud on living and creating from your higher consciousness (genius); and I climbed to the summit of Mount Kilimanjaro with people I met during my training in Africa, to raise funds for a children's home in Kenya and to fulfill a long-time dream of mine.

Yet, as transformational as my time in Swaziland was, the call to Africa was not the first message from my soul that has taken me down this path of hanging out with visionary people. Before Africa there was India, and my encounter with a person I can only describe as an Italian version of Gandhi.

As you'll see in this chapter, in the stories of a visionary leader I met in India and an entrepreneurial mom from San Diego empowering women and girls in Uganda, once you are focused in the pursuit of a vision, the next steps are to tap into your inner guidance, be open to unexpected opportunities, and have the courage to follow your truth. While the journey may be challenging, its rewards for you and all those you touch will far exceed the effort.

Letting Inner Guidance Illuminate the Path

Roaming through one of India's ancient towns, Sarnath, where Buddha once taught, I hoped he was guiding me as I followed a dusty red dirt road past mud houses, stray cows, and a few seemingly stray children, to a highly unusual school. I was invited to tour the school and interview one of its cofounders, Valentino Giacomin, for a book I was writing about visionary change-makers—and now this book, as well. A former teacher and journalist in Italy, Valentino came to India to establish the Alice Project Universal Education School—and to inspire a whole new educational paradigm. So he certainly fit my definition of an agent of global change.

I arrived in a colorful courtyard dominated by a huge Buddhist stupa (shrine), to the sounds of children chanting mantras in their open-air classrooms. As I waited for Valentino, I was met by the bright smiles and greetings ("Ciao," "Namaste," "Hello") of six-year-

VALENTINO GIACOMIN, a former teacher and journalist from Italy, cofounded the Alice Project Universal Education School with fellow Italian teacher Luigina De Biasi. After a serendipitous meeting with His Holiness the Dalai Lama, who encouraged him to combine spiritual practices with education, Valentino bought a piece of land in Sarnath, India, in 1994 and built a school that would integrate the practice of universal spirituality with traditional curricula. Including the original school—officially recognized by the Indian government—Valentino has now set up three schools in India for underprivileged children. Located in the states of Uttar Pradesh (where the Sarnath school is), Bihar, and Arunachal Pradesh, all follow the Alice Project methodology.

For more information, visit *www.aliceproject.org*

4

olds to teenagers. The only thing that shined brighter than their smiles was the light in their eyes—a light, suggestive of confidence, that even the Dalai Lama was said to have noticed when he visited the school.

Imagine a school of about a thousand students, where there was not one case of attention deficit/hyperactivity disorder, and bullying did not exist. That was the Alice Project. Here, children from every faith studied language and sciences, as well as spiritual practices such as meditation, mindfulness, and yoga. Both the school and Valentino's vision for education fascinated me.

So exactly how did an Italian teacher, raised as a Catholic, end up establishing a universal school in rural northern India? Two life-changing events were instrumental in Valentino's awakening and in his answering the call to his own hero's journey.

Answering the Call

The first event happened when, at one point in his career, Valentino found himself without a job, money, or security. He decided to find a solution, not in a new job but in "seeking happiness." He became interested in yoga, which at the time he knew nothing about. He also knew nothing about Hindu or Buddhist philosophy.

His intuition, nevertheless, led him to a Buddhist center, where he heard a lama (monk) talk about health, suffering, and the many different kinds of "hells." Having grown up in the Western Christian tradition, where there existed only one hell, Valentino was skeptical about the lama's teaching and couldn't grasp what he was talking about. Then a young monk approached him and said, "Just look at your mind—that's where many 'hells' exist."

That was Valentino's big "aha" moment—the instant he understood that the lama was talking not about external hells but about something that happens in consciousness. It was a turning point for him when he realized that everything came from the mind. Buddhism changed Valentino's life and became a springboard for his own awakening. As a teacher, he envisioned bringing Buddhism into the curricula of schools to introduce a balance between study and spiritual practice.

He started implementing some of the core ideas of Buddhism in his classroom in Italy. He met fellow teacher Luigina De Biasi, and together they experimented with a new methodology in three Italian government schools before bringing the strategy to India. They wanted to shake the foundation of old knowledge and to "rethink everything." The experiment became known as the Alice Project.

"Alice" in the school's name refers to the young heroine of Lewis Carroll's classic story, *Alice's Adventures in Wonderland,* who takes a brave trip down the "rabbit hole" to explore her own inner world and subconscious. Alice embodies the courageous and somewhat solitary journey we all must take to explore and understand our inner landscape so that we are better able to influence the outer one.

Pursuing His Truth

The second life-changing event for Valentino occurred in 1988, when he met His Holiness the Dalai Lama in the hillside city of Dharamsala, the Dalai Lama's home in India, and seized the opportunity for some high-level life coaching. "What job should I pursue in my life?" Valentino asked the Dalai Lama. After much contemplation, His Holiness had an answer. As Valentino recalls, the advice from the Dalai Lama was, "Journalism, not so good, but education...that would be excellent, excellent." Then he suggested that Valentino combine his spiritual practice and career in education by coming to India!

When Valentino listened to his own inner knowing—and the guidance from the Dalai Lama—he found his truth: teaching children to explore their own way to inner peace. Then it was just a question of *where*. In 1994, Valentino made his dream a reality when, at age 50, he bought a piece of land in the town of Sarnath. There he built India's first Alice Project Universal Education School, combining academic studies with spiritual practices. Auspiciously, it was just a short walk from the deer park in Sarnath where Buddha first taught and delivered the Four Noble Truths, the central concepts of Buddhist thought.

Like a modern-day Gandhi with an Italian edge, Valentino embodied peace and compassion in his actions—exactly what the students of the Alice Project learned to do as well through their daily practices of meditation and mindfulness.

Valentino saw the Alice Project as a model or pilot project for other schools everywhere. Though the school's approach includes spirituality, it is not about religion, Valentino says. "At the Alice Project, we teach students *how* to think, not *what* to think. The teaching is based on a holistic view of the world. We teach students about the mind and how it works. Each child's journey is his or her own. We'll guide the car and teach them how to drive, but where they go is up to them."

What began with only 75 students and four teachers now involves more than 1,200 students, 45 teachers, and three schools—located in Sarnath, a city in Uttar Pradesh; in Bodh Gaya, a religious site in Bihar; and in a village in the northern state of Arunachal Pradesh.

In this environment of joy and mindfulness, Alice Project students perform well academically and, according to a study done by a professor at Banaras Hindu University, have greater attentiveness, memory, awareness, and discipline than students from other Indian schools. This practice of "external education meets inner peace," if adopted elsewhere, could change the face of education far beyond the borders of India.

In following his own truth and answering the call to come to India, Valentino Giacomin embarked on a spiritual path that paralleled the Alice Project's philosophy: An inner journey and exploration can help you understand—and alter—your external circumstances. Directed by his own inner guidance system, Valentino answered the call of his soul and found the courage and resources to create his vision of a new way of educating in an ancient land—igniting great change in his life and in the lives of thousands of children.

Like Valentino, another visionary change agent—this time an entrepreneurial mom from San Diego—answered the call to serve in a faraway country to bring her vision to life.

VIVIAN GLYCK is the founder and executive director of Just Like My Child Foundation, an organization that works to improve the lives of mothers and children around the world and to empower girls to reach their full potential. In 2008, Vivian was honored with the Women of Peace Award, presented by the Women's Peacepower Foundation; in 2013, she was named one of San Diego's 50 People to Watch by *San Diego Magazine* for her philanthropy and work in Africa, specifically in Uganda. In addition to her humanitarian work, Vivian is a successful author, entrepreneur, and marketing director whose clients have included Deepak Chopra, Anthony Robbins, and Dean Ornish.

For more information, visit *www.justlikemychild.org*

Finding Support for a Vision

Vivian Glyck exemplifies our power to create what we love when truth and wisdom converge. Vivian is the founder and executive director of Just Like My Child Foundation, an organization dedicated to improving the lives of mothers and children globally. In fact, she's been described as a "global mama" for her work with women and children in Uganda and, more recently, Senegal. But her dreams for African mothers and their children could not have happened without some amazing synchronicity that helped her find the perfect place and person to support her vision.

It all started with the intense love Vivian experienced when her son was born. She realized that, just like her, mothers around the world fiercely love and want to protect their children. After learning that about every 30 seconds a child in Africa dies from malaria and that about 13 million children have been orphaned by the AIDS epidemic, she awoke one night, sprang from her bed, and said to her husband, "I have to go to Africa."

As crazy as that sounded, she was compelled to answer her soul's call. Her thought was to go to East Africa because of the widespread AIDS issues there, but when an opportunity arose to go to Senegal with the Agape International Spiritual Center in Los Angeles, she jumped at the chance. As destiny would have it, in Senegal she met someone who just happened to be working in East Africa and who directed her to a convent and small medical clinic in rural Uganda.

Six months later, she arrived at the clinic. There, she met Sister Ernestine Akulu, a formidable administrator with a vision of her own for the clinic. She became Vivian's powerful partner in that country. That was in 2006; later that year, Just Like My Child Foundation (JLMC) was born.

Vivian recalls the pure joy in making her first financial contribution on behalf of JLMC. "I'll never forget the very first money I was able to send over to Uganda. It was to buy an electric generator, so they could turn the lights on while they were trying to help these women who were coming in during their last moments of labor to give birth. I went into a Bank of America and said, 'I'm wire-transferring this money over,' and all the tellers in the bank were on their feet and so excited."

Turning a Dream into Reality

From there, Just Like My Child Foundation has developed programs for microenterprise, health care, female empowerment, and legal rights education. They began helping women and children acquire knowledge and tools to deal with poverty, disease, land rights, and the all-too-common traumas of domestic violence and rape. The programs have had a huge impact on the lives of thousands of Ugandan women and families in dozens of villages—and continue to do so.

For example, JLMC's Project Keep a Mother Alive has been restructuring and rebuilding a hospital since 2006. What began as a clinic with no electricity, doctors, medical supplies, bed nets, or malaria treatment is now a flourishing women's hospital in rural Uganda. The hospital has saved the lives of or provided less urgent health care for more than five thousand mothers over the last several years, through AIDS treatment and obstetrical interventions.

Another shining example of creating from your heart is one of Vivian's favorite programs, JLMC's Girl Power Project. It currently teaches hundreds of girls about the issues of early pregnancy and AIDS, how to have the strength to state their rights, and how to be free enough to become educated leaders. Through the Girl Power Project, the organization has a vision to empower one million vulnerable adolescent girls and the communities they live in, to improve the health and economic stability of these areas and thereby improve the health of the whole world. As part of that vision, in 2015, Just Like My Child Foundation joined the Clinton Global Initiative and committed to implement a pilot program for the Girl Power Project that would support ten thousand girls.

"It's huge; it's such an amazing experience to see these girls come to life and feel their power," Vivian has said. "For me, the greatest gift I can give somebody is to see their own possibility and potential burst open." Another big goal of the program is to see the girls from the Girl Power Project graduate from college.

As Vivian noted, perhaps the first female Ugandan president could come out of this group of girls! "It's about holding that vision of what is possible and the kind of transformation that can happen when a woman enters into a leadership position in Africa."

Yes, by holding the vision of what's possible, Vivian and Just Like My Child Foundation have realized phenomenal results in relatively few years. JLMC has empowered more than 200,000 people in 76 communities in Uganda, transforming the lives of thousands of families and helping them break the cycle of poverty. With added financial support, the vision for JLMC now extends far beyond the borders of Uganda. The organization has begun working in two communities in Senegal and over the next few years plans to establish programs in four additional countries.

And all because when Africa called, Vivian Glyck answered.

Lessons to Take with You

All transformation starts with a decision. By answering their soul's calling and pursuing their visionary projects, Valentino Giacomin and Vivian Glyck changed everything—not just their own lives but those of so many others. Support, guidance, and resources all aligned *after* they made that decision.

Don't discard your dreams or dismiss inner nudges. You might discover your life's work, or at least something you'd love to create, by listening to messages from your higher self and choosing what you are drawn to or would love to do. By following your own truth, you make it possible to realize creations that would not otherwise exist on the planet.

Questions for Contemplation

1. What does your heart care about, and why?

2. What are your natural gifts and talents? What makes you come alive when you're involved in it? *(Note: Joy is the "operating mode" when you're following your soul's truth or authentic expression.)*

3. Whom are *you* here to serve, help, or inspire?

4. Is there a call you've been ignoring?

AWAKENING
EMBRACING THE MYSTERY

*"Life will give you whatever experience is most help-
ful for the evolution of your consciousness."*

~ Eckhart Tolle ~

Headlights glaring in my eyes—that's almost all I remember about that pitch-black November night on a small country highway. Just the intensity of the high beams from the oncoming vehicle blinding me as I rounded the curve.

"What's that? I think there's a car in our lane!" I cried out to my sister, who was next to me, in the passenger seat. She had no time to reply.

Darkness. Silence. I awaken on an unusually hard, narrow bed—and then realize it's a gurney. The lights in the room are harsh and the walls stark. I'm in the tiny rural hospital in Treherne, Manitoba, just an hour or two after a drunk driver at the wheel of a van hit my Toyota Celica head-on.

Groggy but conscious, I look up at the nurse standing over me.

"Where's Gracie? How's my sister?"

The nurse's face is white. She is silent, unable to speak as tears well up in her kind eyes.

"She's dead, isn't she?" I whisper, gulping back the emotions swelling in my throat.

"Yes," the nurse says quietly and nods. "She died in the crash. We've called your parents."

My beautiful, 23-year-old sister died instantly, four inches from my side. In my last memory of her, she is talking excitedly about what she planned to do after university. Just moments before those dreams would be crushed. Forever.

I don't even remember the sound of the impact that left my platinum-colored hatchback in a twisted wreckage—glass, steel, and rubber strewn across the highway and a nearby field. I never saw the carnage after the collision, and I thank God that image is not part of my memory bank.

I left the small hospital the next day with my parents, hobbling on my left leg, using crutches to keep the weight off my broken right foot. My body was bruised and battered, and I needed ten stitches in my scalp to close a head wound that resulted from my skull slamming into the steering wheel. Yet, for all intents and purposes, I was fairly intact physically. Emotionally, I was shattered. Few things test our power and ability to go on more than deep physical or emotional trauma.

At my sister's funeral, the air was thick with tragedy, no matter how much we tried to frame it as a "celebration of life." While she lived fully—at least until age 23—with an open heart, a sense of adventure, and a deep love for family and friends, there was an overwhelming feeling that her final breath had come too soon.

My physical injuries healed, miraculously, within a few months, but the emotional loss of my sister stayed with me for years. She had embodied her name, Grace—beauty in form and character, inside and out—and I missed her immensely.

I knew I'd survived the massive collision for a reason, but that didn't ease the pain. I was constantly reminded of a quote from writer Richard Bach: "Here is a test to find whether your mission on earth is finished: If you're alive, it isn't." Perhaps all people with great vision and purpose know this—or maybe they just persevere through physical, mental, or financial hardship because they simply refuse to give up. In most, if not all, cases, they succeed in creating what they want because they have extraordinary tenacity and will.

That life-altering car accident tested but did not defeat my will. Yet it wasn't until I could embrace the mystery of what happened—and not need to know "why"—that I could move forward again.

Embracing the Mystery

Life is fragile, unpredictable, and often unexplainable. Most of us get that. But it's only when we can move through life's events without needing or demanding an explanation that we can endure, and even transcend, challenges—and carry on with creating the life we want.

Several years after the car accident that killed my sister, I went to see a spiritual healer for guidance. I thought I had "dealt with" my sister's death, but apparently, my subconscious had not. In an emotional session, I received this message from my spiritual guide:

> There is deep mystery in choosing to incarnate on the earth plane. You have chosen to be part of a deep mystery—one that has caused you very deep pain. Contemplate the possibility that by embracing the mystery, knowing that you cannot wrap a rational mind around it, you can let it go and embrace the mystery at a soul level. There is something beyond the rational. On a soul level there is always a connec-

tion; on a physical level, the loss is real. Honor that. Respect that. But at the same time, remember and understand that not all will be grasped rationally.

Understand that not all will be grasped rationally. Wow. That was a lot to ask. How do we embrace life and let it unfold without needing to know what will happen next? Aren't we wired (and taught) always to be setting goals and planning for the future?

That's what I thought until I met an incredible individual who had also experienced a horrendous car accident in which he lost loved ones. Despite this trauma, he allowed his life, and his vision to raise human consciousness, to unfold in a profound way.

A Moment of Awakening

Roman emperor and philosopher Marcus Aurelius said, "Accept whatever comes to you woven in the pattern of your destiny, for what could more aptly fit your needs?" It's hard to imagine that a life-altering tragedy would fit anyone's "needs," but when a circumstance seems insurmountable, it is necessary to look at it—and live through it—from another, higher, perspective.

This is what Matthew Sanford did after surviving a traumatic car accident when he was just 13. On the night that changed his life forever,

MATTHEW SANFORD is a nationally recognized yoga instructor and workshop leader, teaching at yoga conferences, studios, and institutions across the United States. A car accident left him paralyzed at age 13, but in 2002, Matthew founded Mind Body Solutions, an organization that offers traditional and adaptive yoga classes to people dealing with trauma, loss, and disability. He invites these individuals to awaken to their potential through the mind-body connection. An inspiring speaker and author, Matthew shares his message and his personal story on stages across the country, as well as in his award-winning book, *Waking: A Memoir of Trauma and Transcendence.*

For more information, visit *www.mindbodysolutions.org*

Matthew's whole family was in the vehicle. His father was driving, and Matthew, who was in the backseat with his two siblings, had gone to sleep leaning against his sister.

Suddenly, the car hit some ice, careened, and skidded off an embankment. Matthew's father and sister were killed instantly. His mother and brother didn't sustain any physical injuries, but Matthew was thrown from the car and broke his neck at vertebra C1. He also broke his back and both of his wrists. His lungs filled with fluid, and he sustained injuries to his pancreas that left him unable to eat for nearly 60 days. He went from 119 pounds to just 79 pounds.

Matthew was paralyzed from the chest down. The doctors told him that any sensation below his point of injury was forever gone and that his only option was to make his upper body stronger so that he could drag his paralyzed body through life—that was their vision for him. Essentially, they painted a picture in which Matthew could be a floating upper torso, compensating for his incapacitated lower body, and somehow making his life work. He was taught that he was no longer connected to his body below the spinal injury, and that his paralysis was simply "a loss." For 12 years after the accident, he believed just that.

But by the time Matthew reached 25, he really missed his body. He had been an athletic kid and wanted desperately to live in his whole body again. He had to find another way to "feel" his body, even though his doctors had told him a dozen years earlier it couldn't be done. He started practicing yoga.

As Matthew explored a different kind of mind-body connection from the one his doctors had predicted, he began an incredible journey. Although he couldn't move his legs, he felt an awareness—an extremely subtle sensation—that traveled through his *whole* body despite his not being able to flex certain muscles. Matthew's exploration of his injury and paralysis revealed that a level of vibrancy still exists in what is typically perceived as a loss of sensation. He discovered that the brain receives more sensory messages from the body than we typically pay attention to. In fact, when he deeply explored the mind-body relationship, he discovered a tingling that transcended even a severed spinal cord.

That sensation, which he could feel throughout his whole body, became the cornerstone of his yoga practice. And while he wasn't exactly sure how it happened, he knew he could teach it. That became Matthew's vision: to be a pioneer in adapting yoga for people living with disabilities. In 2002, he founded Mind Body Solutions, an organization that provides yoga classes to people dealing with trauma, loss, or disability, to help them reconnect with their bodies and find greater peace and healing.

Like other instructors, Matthew has taught yoga and led workshops at studios around the United States; unlike others, Matthew teaches yoga from a wheelchair. And he has often taught students who, *unlike* him, can stand and walk.

Now 51, Matthew has been exploring the mind-body relationship for over 25 years. In addition to being able to teach yoga to others with or without disabilities, he has discovered that he can feel things most people who can walk *can't* feel. Without as much distraction, and with no muscular control or ability to walk, he has found a hum, what he calls the inner hum of consciousness, within his paralysis. It's as if he can "hear" someone tickling the bottoms of his feet.

The discovery of this sensation does not necessarily mean Matthew will walk again. But it does mean he can live vibrantly through his whole body.

The Mystery Embraced

Let's review. When Matthew's back broke, he was knocked out of two-thirds of his body. Two months after the accident, he was told that any sensation he got in his legs below his point of injury was nothing more than a phantom feeling, as if his legs had been amputated.

Instead of believing that he had no sensation, Matthew started to "listen" to the sensation of paralysis—literally to what it felt like *inside* his paralysis. And it turned out that despite his paralysis, he was still able to perceive meaningful sensation. Matthew believed in his *own* experience of this heightened level of presence and mind-body connection. When realized, this sensation not only opened up the possibility of greater spiritual peace but also had practical benefits.

That's the work of Mind Body Solutions today—helping people discover this subtle level of sensation through deepening their mind-body relationship. In working with people who have spinal injuries, Matthew helps them identify and learn how to move this subtle energy through their body. They can improve their ability to transfer from a wheelchair to a bed or a chair, for example, by learning how to transfer *energy*.

Matthew says, "You can try to will yourself through, pushing yourself where you want to go, but if you can feel it from the inside out, that's transformation."

Mind Body Solutions has trained yoga teachers from around the United States, Canada, and Europe in how to teach the principles of yoga to anybody—with or without a disability.

Matthew found, "When you become aware and connect deeper within the inner body, it also shifts and connects you more deeply to the people and world around you. Mind-body awareness is more than a personal health strategy. It's a shift in consciousness." Through yoga, Matthew embraced the mystery between mind and body and made it his life's work to explore and use it as a tool for healing. From teaching yoga in a wheelchair to establishing an organization based on mind-body principles that is healing thousands, Matthew has been able to embrace the unknown and bring his vision into the world.

And he's not finished. As he says in his book, *Waking: A Memoir of Trauma and Transcendence*, "I believe this shared connection has profound implications not just for the shape and quality of our consciousness, but for the aging process, for the experience of trauma, for our approach to disability and rehabilitation, and even for our survival on this planet."

When you create your own vision of what's possible, not what others tell you is possible, and embrace the mystery beyond rational thought, you are operating from higher consciousness, the place of imagination, insight, and the unknown—the place where miracles happen.

Lessons to Take with You

The more expansive your thoughts and the more powerful your ability to embrace the unknown, the more expansive the life and reality you can envision and create. Imagination and the ability to move beyond the rational are critical in shaping what's possible, regardless of circumstances and other people's beliefs, opinions, or experiences.

Powerful people understand and honor their emotions but do not bow to them; they carry on and create from a place of mystery and discovery rather than logic, limitation, or explanation.

Questions for Contemplation

1. What challenges do you face in your life?

2. What are some alternative ways to perceive or handle these challenges?

3. How might you embrace some of life's experiences without the need to understand or explain them?

ALCHEMY
TURNING LEAD INTO GOLD

"Remember that all things which happen
To you are raw materials
Endlessly fertile

Endlessly yielding of thoughts that could change
Your life and go on doing forever....

So fear not, my friend.
The darkness is gentler than you think."

~ Ben Okri ~

Sometimes, a breakdown is necessary for a break*through*. Just as alchemists attempted to break down lead in order to transmute it to gold, in life, old patterns and structures must be dissolved to make way for the new.

I had my midlife crisis early—at 25. I'd just returned from a year of working, traveling, and exploring the landscape—and men—of Australia, and another four months traipsing around the sites of Southeast Asia. My journey was like one of those free-spirited backpacking trips other 20-somethings take through Europe, but it offered slightly more extreme contrasts and adventures—like 44ºC (111ºF) heat in the Outback of Australia; learning to scuba dive among sharks and stingrays on the Great Barrier Reef; and exploring the ancient cultures and modern mysteries of places like Taipei, Bangkok, Tokyo, and Ubud (Bali).

When I left for the other side of the world, I had already finished a four-year bachelor of nursing degree and had worked for two years as a registered nurse in an adrenaline-charged neonatal unit with premature and sick newborns. I was ready for a break—from grueling, 12-hour shifts—and in search of adventure, culture shock, and perhaps an earthshaking romance. That's what I really longed to discover ten thousand miles away, in the other hemisphere of the world, somewhere on South Pacific shores.

After an amazing 16 months of foreign travel, I returned to reality in conventional, predictable Winnipeg, Canada. I had more than the post-travel blues—I hated my life, if you could call it a life, and longed for the change and daily unexpectedness of my time on the road. At 25, I felt alone (at least in my mind), empty, and directionless. I had a loving family, a few close friends, and a place to call a temporary home, but none of that seemed to move the needle on my happiness meter.

In what seemed like a good idea at the time, I decided to change my job, home, and province; I headed west to Edmonton, Alberta, to revive my nursing career in a new field, coronary care, where the patients are basically heart attacks waiting to happen. Bad move. What I thought would make me come alive again almost killed me.

Working as a rookie coronary care nurse was too intense for me; I was used to treating sick babies, not 200-pound adults with unstable hearts. I spent hours poring over electrocardiogram readings trying to detect abnormal heart rhythms before a patient went into "V-fib" (ventricular fibrillation, the heart's fast track to death);

learning the correct dosages of lidocaine, adrenaline, potassium, and about a hundred other lifesaving drugs; and being on constant watch for any cardiac crisis.

Sinking into Depression

Enduring this intense job, filled with actual life-and-death decisions, compounded with living in a new city with few friends, I found my stress level was off the charts; I'm sure my adrenal glands were working overtime. I became anxious and started showing up for work early and leaving late, turning 12-hour shifts into 16-hour days, including the commute. I was stressed to the max, sleep-deprived, dead on my feet, and starting to lose my concentration. Sleep deprivation can be brutal that way. I was terrified I'd make a mistake, and a patient—who already had a weak heart—would suffer the consequences. That never happened, but the possibility of it haunted my every waking hour. Being the studious nurse I was, I knew the major symptoms of depression—and I realized I had most of them.

I spiraled downward into depression, exacerbated by insomnia. Trying to save lives on two to four hours of sleep a night left me exhausted. And my nonexistent social life meant even my "downtime" just brought me further down. I wanted rest. Deep rest. Peace. The ability to function like a semi-normal human being again. But I didn't have the physical, mental, or spiritual strength to make the changes necessary to feel well again. I couldn't turn the tide; I was drowning emotionally. I was so-o-o beaten down. I wanted out. I was ready to leave the planet—I hated my life, and myself, that much.

Shocked that my mental health had plummeted so far, so fast, my brother took me to see a psychiatrist at the University of Alberta Hospital's emergency room. A soft-spoken, middle-aged shrink said yes, I was depressed, and suggested I return to Winnipeg, where I had more support and could get treatment. I immediately resigned from my position as a cardiac-care nurse and flew back to the city I had so desperately tried to escape. All I could think was, *What the hell is wrong with me? Why can't I pull my life together?*

It was January, in Manitoba, and the extreme climate meant −40°C (−40°F) temperatures, and short, dark days. My inner landscape was just as bleak. This move had not exactly been the perfect remedy to lift my spirits. With its effects heightened by my somber mood, the atmosphere seemed so intense—so impenetrable.

I remember walking into my parents' pink bathroom (trendy décor in the '60s) and thinking that even the rose-colored walls seemed a deep shade of intense. No matter where I looked or what I did, nothing lifted the veil of my despair. My emotions were spent, my mind empty, my soul numb.

I continued to contemplate suicide but never actually attempted it, as much as I wanted out of this dark, never-ending tunnel. The thought of what it would do to my mom kept me from a premature exit. In retrospect, I might have been healed by meditation, yoga, and rest—but these weren't conventional approaches at the time.

When the suicidal thoughts and sleep deprivation persisted, it meant another trip to the emergency room, this time at Victoria General Hospital in Winnipeg. The psychiatrist on call was a thoughtful, caring young MD with a sense of humor. In the end, "Dr. G." would be a life raft of humor, caring, and compassion in the unstable seas of the psych ward.

I was diagnosed with depression (no surprise there) and voluntarily admitted to the psychiatric unit, with liberal evening and weekend passes to go home. I was terrified. This was not how I saw my life evolving at age 25. I thought, *Isn't this supposed to be the* PRIME *of my life? Where had I taken a wrong turn onto this downward spiral staircase?*

Life hurt—badly. I had never known such debilitating, profound sadness, sadness that could kill you, or at least make you *want* to die.

I wanted out. A way out of the pain. Yet I moved between feeling sad and feeling nothing—numb. At those times, I wanted to feel *something* again—*anything*. I was caught between worlds. I wondered, *Should I stay or should I go?* I knew I needed help. I also knew that while I might be depressed, I was *not* crazy.

I spent about three months in and out of the psych ward, prescribed the usual plethora of Western medicine's drugs and treatments for depression—MAO inhibitors (antidepressants), lithium, group therapy, and lots of mundane activities like baking, arts and crafts, and exercise routines suitable for senior citizens. For me, the treatment of the illness was even more painful than its symptoms.

That said, as my depression deepened, my awareness somehow heightened. I was able to observe my own mental state from a higher lookout point, where I could watch what was happening without being "in it." My stint in the psych ward became a clinical self-study in the power of the mind. On one hand, my cognitive function was so shut down that I couldn't write my own name—I knew it but couldn't form the letters. On the other hand, I was having out-of-body experiences and episodes during which I felt like I was time-traveling. I found these events to be weird and extremely powerful at the same time.

However, amid the extremely low energy of the psych unit (and I'm not just talking about the patients), my profound sense of despair and disconnection got worse. Everything—my environment, my body, and especially the people around me—felt separate and outside of me. I spent as much time as I could alone, weeping softly to simply let the pain flow out of me.

During those three dark months, there were only two places I could find peace and solitude—my parents' home and the hospital chapel. Both gave me the space to be alone, and both had the vibration of unconditional love. I could actually feel the higher energy in those places, where I was almost able to feel like my old, happier self. Even my psychiatrist noticed how much "better" I was after returning from a weekend at home. I told him it was because I felt love there. In the hospital ward, I felt terror, negativity, and instability.

The Moment of Transformation

Western medicine was not lifting me from my despair, and in many ways, it was compounding my dark and depressed state. One particularly low day, at my wit's end and madly chasing peace, I decided God and I needed to talk. I went to the hospital chapel and sat in the front pew. If God, a higher power, or some reasonable facsimile did exist, now was the time to make itself known. My soul ached for a reason to stay on the earth plane. If I didn't get some kind of sign—soon—I was going to exit the planet and end this ongoing struggle.

I began my conversation with God, and let him know that I was serious about wanting to die and ending my seemingly intractable emotional pain. From the bottom of my heart, I asked for a sign that God, or some form of infinite being, actually existed.

Immediately, an indescribable sensation of lightness moved through my body. *If there is such a thing as Christ consciousness, this must be what it feels like,* I thought. And if Jesus's spirit wasn't with me at that moment, then it definitely was that of one of his trusted representatives.

"You're *real,*" I whispered. At the time, I didn't know anything about chakras; connecting with high vibrational energy; or just "Being," as Eckhart Tolle writes about in *The Power of Now.* But if I had, I would have guessed that my crown chakra had opened right up to become a channel for a higher, deeply loving energy that moved through my whole body like a gentle wave of soft light. Suddenly, my fear fell away, and so did the desire to die.

My soul spoke. God answered. And I received the message loud and clear. God/Spirit/Source/the Force—call it what you will—*is real.* I had tapped into my higher consciousness, that pure state of awareness connected to all of time and space, where you have no identity and you are "one with the universe." I have never forgotten that moment; to say it was transformational would be a huge understatement.

In his book *Power vs. Force,* David R. Hawkins says that the levels of consciousness have different vibrational frequencies, with love, joy, peace, and enlightenment correlating to the highest energy levels. Hawkins says, "As Love becomes more and more unconditional, it begins to be experienced as inner Joy." This doesn't refer to the joy experienced during pleasurable events or activities but to a deep level of healing and state of compassion. In this energy field, Hawkins says, "A Presence is felt whose power facilitates phenomena outside conventional expectations of reality, termed *miraculous* by the ordinary observer." The energy and presence I experienced that day felt just like that—miraculous. Otherworldly. Indescribable.

It felt like a thousand pounds of grief, loss, and anguish had been lifted from my shoulders and replaced with deep peace. Tears streamed down my face. I knew everything from then on would be okay. I checked out of the hospital—for good—just days later.

"Acute unhappiness can be a great awakener," Eckhart Tolle has said. My journey through my dark side, what I had perceived as a spiritual crisis, became a profound awakening and healing experience. In the end, I was able to transmute the "lead" in my unconscious into a huge amount of spiritual gold.

While mine was a decidedly inward process of finding light in the darkness, two modern-day visionaries you'll meet in this chapter transformed external "dark elements," such as violence, fear, and gang activity, into expressions of art, love, and peace. One, an inspiring, multidisciplinary artist, did it from her front porch; the other, a former-businessman-turned-youth-mentor, did it from the inner-city neighborhoods of Los Angeles. The first is Vanessa German, who transformed a violent neighborhood in Pittsburgh by teaching art in her front yard and using love and creativity as catalysts for change. The latter is Tony LoRe, who is also using the power of love and adult guidance to change the lives of at-risk young people in crime-ridden parts of Los Angeles.

Responding to Violence

Sometimes, you don't have to travel far to find and fulfill your vision. Photographer, poet, actress, sculptor, designer, and educator Vanessa German grew up in Homewood, Pennsylvania, cited as one of the most violent neighborhoods in the United States. Public-Source, a Pennsylvania news organization, identifies Homewood as one of the deadliest areas in Pittsburgh, with the highest homicide rate in the city from 2010 to 2013. Vanessa has had a close experience of the violence there: "I have friends whose sons have been shot and killed, shot and wounded, or shot and in prison."

One day, she was relaxing on her front porch when she heard 21 gunshots. She waited. She worried—about her neighbors, the victims, and their families. And then she took action. Those gunshots became the impetus for a campaign of love in her neighborhood—first with signs, then with art—which was not planned but which certainly had an impact.

VANESSA GERMAN is the founder of Love Front Porch, an organization she started to encourage at-risk youth to create art—right on her porch—in an effort to reduce violence and gang-related activity in her inner-city neighborhood. A multidisciplinary artist based in Pittsburgh, Vanessa believes art has the power to heal. A photographer, poet, actress, sculptor, designer, and educator, Vanessa was named by the Pittsburgh Center for the Arts as its 2012 Emerging Artist of the Year.

Deeply affected by the violence in her neighborhood, including its impact on friends and family, she refused to sit by and believe there was nothing she could do. She started thinking about how she could use her gifts, talents, and resources to make a difference.

One idea came from seeing signs for political candidates around the area. She began printing yard signs with messages of nonviolence, such as, "Stop Shooting: We Love You." First she put them up in her yard. Then she distributed them around the neighborhood— all two hundred of the initial batch. The signs caught on, and eight hundred more now appeared all the way from her neighborhood into the city of Pittsburgh and beyond!

But Vanessa didn't stop there. In an effort to reduce violence and gang-related activity in the area, she began creating art with at-risk youth on her front porch. She started by letting people see what she did. When the weather was nice, she'd sculpt with clay on her porch. Kids in the neighborhood and people standing at the corner bus stop would see her doing something messy and fun, and some would lean on her fence to watch her work. They also plied her with questions: "What are you building?" "Who told you that you could do that?" "Did you go to school to do that?" "Can we do it, too?"

Soon the children wanted not only to see but also to touch Vanessa's artwork. And they wanted to create something they loved, too. Children started jumping Vanessa's fence into her yard. She let them work on her sculptures and do simple things, but it was never enough for them. So one day she invited them to make art with her— and the porch filled up.

Every day, more and more kids came, craving art. Vanessa knew the art was having a positive effect, because the same kids who used to play "gang" in the alleyways behind her house were now showing up at her door. She and her partner pulled out all the old paint and brushes from the basement, as well as any other art supplies they could find. She let the budding artists paint on anything—bricks, chunks of slate, pieces of old paneling, old T-shirts. The yard—and front porch—spilled over with paint-splattered kids, dancing and singing while they created their masterpieces.

Tapping into the Power of Love

Love Front Porch began as a kind of impromptu art studio in 2012, with neighborhood children and adults just watching Vanessa work and create art outdoors. But as the art and the number of young artists grew, it was clear they needed more space. Vanessa found a vacant house nearby and got permission to use what became known as the Art House. Basically, Love Front Porch moved under a bigger roof a couple of doors down. It has had an effect on the children and the neighborhood, says Vanessa, as a place to be both creative and at peace.

Vanessa found that making art makes children more compassionate: They communicate with each other; they take care of each other. Some kids use the Art House as a place to find peace after having a bad day at school. Some kids come in and just cry. They need a place where they know they are safe to express their emotions. Vanessa makes sure the children know that the house is an art space, not a fighting space—a place where people take care of each other. "We make art, and we eat snacks. That's what happens here. Every day that the Art House is open, caring, tenderness, and healing happen."

When Vanessa established Love Front Porch, she realized that art was the language of her soul's hands and eyes, and the clearest way she could connect with herself and others. And that deep connection—to her own spirit and soul—is the vision she wanted to share. She says:

> Literally, the hours that pass when I am creating are
> the most love-saturated times of my life. It is the time
> when I am able to most clearly understand myself

and delve into my strengths, my weaknesses, and my fears. If anything, I have hope that the children, and even some of the adults, some of the parents, who come into the Art House will be able to have these moments where they are connected to themselves—to their souls, hearts, and spirits—and no one is making them feel ashamed or stupid. I'm not thinking about what the Art House accomplishes because, really, every day that it happens, love happens.

In a neighborhood that is underserved, depressed, and often dangerous, where people don't think much about the kids, Vanessa knew a space like the Art House could be life-changing: "To have this space where so much love, hope, care, and tenderness are generated is something that is powerful and continues to reveal itself. Every day the house is open, it reveals to me all of what is possible. And all I did was to share the thing I love. Art is love. Love is power." She established Love Front Porch as a platform for kids to learn to create what they love, and share their love, in an area that so desperately needs it.

An alchemist and an artist, Vanessa used the power of her love to transform an atmosphere of violence into a neighborhood where love and acceptance could flourish. At the same time, she inspired the creativity and kindness of her young protégés as well as an entire community.

The Pittsburgh Center for the Arts named Vanessa its 2012 Emerging Artist of the Year, and she has performed at the Carnegie Museum of Art in Pittsburgh. Her sculptures have been shown at the Andy Warhol Museum in Pittsburgh, in New York City galleries, and in exhibits across the United States.

Doing What You *Must* Do

Tony LoRe has also "turned lead into gold." He has inspired thousands of young people and transformed a community by creating safe spaces where at-risk youth can express themselves without fear or judgment.

Tony didn't choose his life's work, he says; it chose him. At one time, Tony was a businessman and successful marketing consultant who also ran baseball camps in the summer for underprivileged kids in Los Angeles. As a result, he was asked to volunteer his time and business skills to run an entrepreneurial program for a small group of students at a high school in South Central Los Angeles. As one thing led to another, soon he was mentoring 17 kids from some of the city's poorest neighborhoods and changing the course of their lives. "Those kids stole my heart," Tony says. Those relationships prompted him to sell his business and dedicate his life to mentoring at-risk youth and transforming a culture of violence and marginalization.

The day Tony decided to pursue his life's work, he remembers seeing this quote from novelist Ursula K. Le Guin: "And the truth is that as a man's real power grows and his knowledge widens, ever the way he can follow grows narrower: until at last he chooses nothing, but does only and wholly what he must do." Decision made. Tony knew what he must do, and in 2001, he founded Youth Mentoring. He continues today as the organization's CEO, designing and running its programs, counseling youth, and collaborating with other nonprofit groups and corporate sponsors. In 15 years, through its various programs as well as trainings with other agencies, Youth Mentoring has created about five thousand mentor-mentee relationships, working mostly with teenagers and high school students but also with children as young as ten.

TONY LoRE is the CEO and founder of Youth Mentoring, a Los Angeles-based organization dedicated to connecting at-risk, inner-city youth with adult mentors in their community. Formerly a successful entrepreneur and marketing consultant, Tony sold his business in 1997, after years of volunteering, to mentor youth in entrepreneurial and other programs full-time. He realized he had found his life's work. Youth Mentoring, established in 2001, began as a small program mentoring just over 40 youths per year. Over the course of 15 years, the organization has created about five thousand mentor-mentee relationships. Tony has also written life skills and business skills curricula for high schools, and he has developed programs and training in entrepreneurism for the Community for Education Foundation. Today he leads Youth Mentoring's programs and services, facilitates youth retreats, and provides mentor trainings to organizations throughout Southern California.

For more information, visit

www.youthmentoring.org

Transforming Wounds into Gifts

In what could be seen as a type of alchemy, turning lower energy into a higher good, Youth Mentoring's model for working with youth is "seeing the gifts that sit next to the wounds." In other words, by seeing young people for who they truly are while acknowledging the pain that exists beneath their fearful or violent actions, mentors can help redirect that behavior to find its gift, or usefulness. According to Tony, this "gift-centered" approach to mentoring operates on the belief that "everybody is born with a unique purpose, and unique gifts to accomplish that purpose. If we approach our youth on this basis," he says, "it counteracts the messages most marginalized kids get every day, that is, 'You don't belong here.'"

Tony found that many youths are *watched* for what they're doing *wrong*—in stores, on the streets, and in school—rather than *seen* for what they're doing *right*. Youth Mentoring adopted an African expression, *Sawubona,* which means "I see you," as its greeting and as the essence of its programs. Mentors use this expression often, so youth understand that the adults are there to "see" their gifts and who they really are, not to judge them or tell them how they should behave.

In a sense, Youth Mentoring welcomes the young people's misbehaviors because these are usually better signs or expressions of their gifts than what they do when they are conforming, says Tony. "Our hearts go out to the exiles and outcasts." For example, one of the mentees was caught leading a ring of young men stealing cell phones. Tony went to visit him in juvenile hall and rather than give him the usual "If you keep this up, you'll end up in prison" speech, Tony said, "You're amazing. How did you get six other guys to do something so stupid?" They ended up having a long conversation about the young man's leadership and persuasion skills. Without condoning his actions, Tony helped him establish that he actually had gifts—as a leader and communicator—and could redirect his behavior to more positive pursuits. That was years ago, and the young man never returned to juvenile detention or ended up in prison. Today, he still participates in many Youth Mentoring programs.

Youth Mentoring's programs center on the idea of community, something Tony has found sadly missing in today's society. "Gangs exist because our youth don't feel connected, or have anything to belong to," Tony says. "We've reduced gang violence with our work simply because we give them a better gang to be part of."

The organization's programs and events establish instant community through the use of cohorts. Twenty-five youths are matched with twenty-five adults who meet as a group on a regular basis. Mentors are trained to guide the group as a whole and mentor all of the youth, not just their individual mentees. For some of these youth, says Tony, this is the first time they've had a community that cares about them.

Four-day retreats in the mountains, another element of the Youth Mentoring model, also empower and unite young people as they experience rites of passage based on indigenous traditions, including drumming, stories, and teachings around a fire. These retreats offer a place for the youth to release their energy, good or bad, and cases of vandalism, fighting, and other gang-type behavior can happen. Rather than resist this bad behavior, the mentors create a safe space that allows it to a point before they intervene to stop or redirect it, again from the approach that Tony calls "gifts and wounds." For example, if a fight breaks out, mentors will step in and show that there are better ways to demonstrate loyalty to a friend (the gift) than through violence (the expression of their wound). "You can't help at-risk youth without taking risks," says Tony. "We just manage the risk."

The risk-taking, caring, and sense of community at Youth Mentoring have shown some impressive results. Many of the youth come from poor neighborhoods with high school graduation rates as low as 27 percent; about 96 percent of the young people in Youth Mentoring graduate from high school.

Programs bring youth and mentors together in everything from surfing lessons to filmmaking to attending events with entrepreneurs. Tony has seen former gang members go to college. A young girl produced a short film about her earlier messed-up life before going on to college, and another former mentee ended up working at the National Security Agency.

Tony's vision was to create an organization that didn't ask young people to change but instead helped them transform the raw materials of their lives into something good—that is, to develop their gifts and purpose in life. Part of that vision is also to inspire a cultural shift and to create a world that sees youth in a different way—one that sees what they are doing right.

"It's the same for all of us as it is for our kids—if you find your gift and live into that, you'll be fulfilled," says Tony. "Your gift isn't that hard to find. When you were in the biggest trouble, what showed up?" And that's how you turn life's lead into gold.

Lessons to Take with You

Emotions correspond to different levels of energy. For example, love has a much higher energetic vibration than fear or hate. Treating others with love, specifically unconditional love, can be a catalyst for change as people experience, connect to, and respond to this higher energy and behave in more positive ways. That is the true "power of love."

Also, limited resources can still effect great change. The most important thing is the first step. Vanessa German started on her front porch; Tony LoRe began mentoring youth in a program at a South Central Los Angeles high school.

See the gifts that exist in each person beneath the pain, fear, or violence being expressed. And look for your own gifts that may sit next to a wound. As the great Sufi poet Rumi said, "The wound is the place where the Light enters you."

Questions for Contemplation

1. What could you be, do, or create that would transmute a low vibrational energy (such as fear or violence) into a high vibrational energy (such as love or creativity)?

2. How can you use the talents, skills, and resources you already have to start realizing a project, vision, or dream?

3. How might you transform or contribute to a community by sharing your "soul gold," starting right where you are?

4. What personal traits or strengths did you summon or draw upon in overcoming a challenge or painful experience? (Note: These qualities may reveal your gifts.)

INTUITION
TAPPING INTO INSIGHTS AND IMAGINATION

*"It is intuition that improves the world, not just
following a trodden path of thought."*

~ Albert Einstein ~

Many visionaries have created their own path for change—where nothing existed before, they have engaged their intuition, imagination, and resources to blaze their own trail and bring their vision to life. At a time when so many of the world's problems seem intractable and impossible to solve, we must focus on creating what we *want* rather than avoiding what we don't. Then the energy shifts from rescuing others to empowering them; in the end, we empower ourselves, too.

This has certainly been the case in my own journey as a global soul. Following my intuition has led to the unfolding of various paths, from a career as an acute-care nurse to becoming a writer, and offered opportunities to live, work, and study on three continents. Moreover, following my intuition has enhanced my ability to be a powerful creative force. Whenever I have engaged both my intuition and my imagination, the wisdom, support, and resources necessary to make my vision a reality appeared.

Here's an example. Years ago, I took a course called "Opening of the Heart," which showed how to tap into your heart's intelligence (aka intuition) to create what you really desire and go where you want—literally and figuratively. At the time, I was carrying on a long-distance relationship with a charming French-Algerian man who lived just outside of Paris. I hadn't envisioned moving to France until my intuition dropped in to say that if the relationship was going to evolve, we needed at least to live in the same country.

I loved France but not the idea of living in Paris or the surrounding area. Again, my inner guidance showed up and suggested I live in the south of France—a slightly outrageous, but better, move. I still had no idea where in the south I'd live, what I could do there, or how I would finance it. Yet again, I tapped into my intuition and was guided to "call my sister," a suggestion that had no logical connection to France. I called her anyway.

"By chance," my sister had just had coffee with a friend who had friends in France who were renting out a house in a tiny village in the heart of Provence. I contacted the couple renting out the house by e-mail and just hours later arranged a year's lease on the residence—including a car—sight unseen. To top it off, the wife was from Winnipeg, my hometown, and she knew of the perfect language school in France where I could brush up on my French. She even sent me an application form for the fall semester!

Within six weeks, I had set up a small adobe house among vineyards, a zippy white Citroën to get around in, and a language school in Aix-en-Provence. The French boyfriend, near Paris, was already in place. Even the finances aligned, through the unexpected sale of some property I owned. My time in Provence was unforgettable—like living in a foreign film for a year.

I could have stayed longer, but guess what: My intuitive guidance directed me back to Winnipeg, where the next big dream awaited.

Following my intuition changed the course of my life. In this chapter, we'll meet an extraordinary doctor who, by following her heart and inner guidance, is changing the course of *humanity*. With help from forces both seen and unseen, Dr. Martina Fuchs has aligned the resources and people necessary to realize an incredible vision of providing disaster relief to thousands, as well as offering holistic health care and better living conditions to millions in some of the world's most impoverished areas.

Following Your Instincts

Dr. Martina Fuchs didn't set out to be a visionary. What started as a desire to provide disaster relief for several months in early 2005, following the Indian Ocean tsunami, unfolded as her life's work. She is the founder and CEO of Real Medicine Foundation (RMF), a global organization that has offered humanitarian programs in 21 countries on five continents.

As a pediatrician trained in Germany and the United States, Martina had always cared deeply about the health and well-being of others, especially chil-

MARTINA FUCHS is the founder and CEO of Real Medicine Foundation, a nonprofit organization that provides humanitarian aid and development to people living in disaster- and poverty-stricken areas, including medical and physical care as well as emotional, economic, and social support. Her work began in 2005 when, as a pediatrician, she set up a small clinic in Sri Lanka to provide relief to the victims of the December 2004 tsunami in Southeast Asia and South Asia. Since then, she and her team have gone beyond disaster relief to help build hospitals and clinics and to provide education, refugee support, and economic initiatives in 21 countries, including Pakistan, the United States, Kenya, Mozambique, Myanmar, Peru, Haiti, Japan, the Philippines, and South Sudan.

For more information, visit *www.realmedicinefoundation.org*

dren. When natural disasters struck around the world, she, like many others, usually donated money and moved on. However, the tsunami of December 26, 2004, was different. This disaster became personal.

When the massive waves wiped out hundreds of thousands of lives in Southeast Asia and South Asia, Martina was in Germany celebrating Christmas with her family, including her two-year-old nephew, Luca. Watching the coverage on television and online, she was completely overwhelmed. She could see that so many of those affected by the tsunami were children Luca's age. They were so little, and they'd lost everything—including their families. She thought, *What if this had happened to someone I love? What if this had happened to Luca, and he suddenly became so vulnerable and exposed to painful things?*

When she returned home to Los Angeles at the end of December, a friend asked if she wanted to go and support the relief efforts somehow. Although Martina had traveled extensively, she had never been in a disaster situation. She had grown up in Germany, and she had worked in some of the most advanced hospitals in Europe and the United States. She had no idea what to expect—and she was somewhat fearful.

The plans with her friend didn't come together, but she knew she had to go to Asia. She had a very strong feeling that told her, *This is the best version of what I can do right now.* So she pushed her fear aside and followed her intuition. Time and money would allow her to help those affected by the tsunami for five or six weeks. That was her plan, and then she would go back to her life. She had no idea that her mission to Asia, inspired by little Luca, would change her life—and her life's purpose—forever.

Moving from Inspiration to Preparation

With so many countries affected by the tsunami, and hundreds of thousands in despair, Martina's next step was to decide where to go.

She reached out to friends, hospitals, and relief organizations in the United States and Europe. She made phone calls to everyone she could think of in the places most deeply affected by the tsunami. Then she put it out to the universe: *Whoever is out there, I need help.*

Apparently, someone was listening. In early January 2005, Martina connected with a friend of a friend, an Australian who had a vacation home in the south of Sri Lanka that had been completely destroyed. The big aid organizations hadn't arrived in the south of Sri Lanka yet, and he said, "Wounds are getting infected and people are in despair. Can you come here?" Martina's intuition spoke: The decision was made. She was on her way to the south of Sri Lanka, specifically the area of Tangalle.

She calculated the medical supplies she would need for five weeks, obtained the necessary vaccinations, and began to create a personal network of support. She flew to Sri Lanka at the end of January, landing in Colombo at night. Traveling south along the coast by car, she witnessed mile after mile of devastation: houses in ruins, people living in tents, and an eerie atmosphere of desolation.

After choosing Sri Lanka and getting there, Martina faced the next challenge: where to begin, and how to contribute in the best way to get the best results. She looked at the only hospital there. It was horrific, with no doctors or supplies; it was dirty, smelly, and clearly lacking in financial support. Many tsunami survivors seeking help at the hospital died there because there were not enough supplies or medical personnel to treat them. A broken leg, left untreated, could lead to bleeding to death. And that happened.

Martina ended up working in one of the large refugee camps near Tangalle called the Mawella Camp, which provided refuge to about a hundred families. Hundreds of other families in the area continued to live in the ruins of their houses along the coast. The villagers asked if she could establish a clinic in the camp. Having only worked in well-equipped, high-tech Western hospitals, Martina had never done such a thing before. But she was determined to use her imagination and "just figure it out" to create something new. "Let's just figure it out" became one of RMF's core principles.

Tapping Imagination

And Martina did figure it out—with an unexpected team of help and talent. There was a structure in the refugee camp that had been hit by the tsunami but not destroyed. Martina didn't see the ruin, however—she imagined the clinic it could become. She recruited young people from the Sri Lanka Navy and people in the camp to help paint the structure and put in windows, doors, and electricity. A woman in the camp sewed curtains. Volunteers from other parts of the world, already in Sri Lanka to help, came to offer their services. A carpenter from Great Britain built Martina an examination table and shelves for medicine and supplies; a plumber from Scotland put in a sink and connected it to a water tank in a nearby tree so the clinic had running water. Martina also discovered an air bridge between Munich and Colombo, by which route medical supplies could be flown for free. Her brother, the head of pediatric surgery at a hospital in Germany, put together seven large boxes of supplies and shipped them by Lufthansa at no cost.

With the clinic up and running, Martina was able to see 70 to 90 patients a day, including children, adults, and pregnant women. The clinic provided access to medical care for about a thousand families living in both the camp and in destroyed homes along the coast.

Martina left Sri Lanka in the middle of March 2005. But she did not go back to her former life as a pediatrician, as she had planned. By the time she left Sri Lanka, she had made promises to raise funds for children who urgently needed heart surgeries, and to set up long-term treatments for several children. Martina applied to establish Real Medicine Foundation (RMF) as a 501(c)(3) nonprofit organization in the United States and the equivalent in Germany, so she could receive support to continue to help in Sri Lanka. In June 2005, she went back to Sri Lanka, and with funding from the organizations in the United States and Europe, she was able to take on more projects. In addition to providing continued support for the Mawella Camp clinic and performing surgeries for many children, she supported an existing preschool and built a new one.

"I did not plan any of this," Martina says. Yet intuitively, she always seemed to know the next action to take. "It really just happened one step at a time."

Pursuing Her Vision

But it didn't stop there. At the end of August 2005, Hurricane Katrina devastated the Gulf Coast of the United States. By then, Real Medicine Foundation was an official nonprofit, and through Martina's magical network of friends, RMF ended up in Memphis to support the 15,000 or so displaced persons there from Mississippi and Louisiana. Then another disaster hit—the Pakistan earthquake in October 2005—and RMF sent volunteer teams of doctors to help about 20,000 people through the winter in the Himalayas. By the end of 2005, from Sri Lanka to the Gulf Coast to Pakistan, humanitarian relief efforts had taken over Martina's life. One natural disaster at a time, Martina's greatest vision was unfolding. And support for the vision appeared at each step.

"Hope is like a path in the countryside. Originally, there is nothing—but as people walk this way again and again, a path appears," said Lu Xun, a Chinese essayist. In many ways, this is how Martina's path has evolved, one idea or insight at a time. Then a helpful friend, resource, or funder appears to support and build upon what's already in place until a clinic, hospital department, or economic program has been created.

By following, trusting, and fine-tuning her intuition, Martina has allowed RMF to flourish. She has learned to listen to, and act upon, that "little voice" of inner guidance. She encourages others to do the same. Several of RMF's projects came as suggestions from the team—someone's intuition and gut instinct saying, *Okay, this is how we could make this happen.* For many projects, RMF sets the foundation for sustainability and moves on. For example, although the organization has worked in 21 countries, it currently has active initiatives in 17.

Real Medicine Foundation focuses on the person as a whole, providing medical, physical, emotional, social, and economic support for the long term. Since 2009, RMF has created a niche in secondary and tertiary health care, which means it has helped to support, upgrade, and operate hospitals, as well as smaller clinics. For example, in 2011, RMF started working with a hospital in northern Kenya that is the only one available for about a million people. RMF began by improving the pediatric department, and then developed it into a teaching and training hospital.

In growing a global organization that now offers humanitarian aid and development to about 15 million people, Martina has tapped into both inner guidance and outer resources to continually affirm her belief that "if you can't find a solution, create one."

Lessons to Take with You

The best way to open and increase your intuition is simply to listen and pay attention to inner voices, hunches, and messages. When you operate from intuition, then ideas, resources, and next actions often align easily. Intuition usually shows you only one or two steps at a time, but taking action brings faster results and success.

Questions for Contemplation

1. Do you tap into your intuition regularly (for example, through meditation) and follow your inner guidance in making important decisions?

2. Where in your life could you ask, *What can I contribute here?* in order to align the resources, people, and support required?

3. Are you making conscious choices, consistently, and taking inspired action to accelerate your success?

PURPOSE
BUILDING (UNSTOPPABLE) MOMENTUM

"The human spirit will not invest itself in a compromise."

~ Robert Fritz ~

When the universe offers you a vision that is bigger, bolder, and more beautiful than what you've ever imagined possible—and you choose to pursue it—your purpose is not something you find, it is something you create. And as you focus on it with all you have, you become *unstoppable*.

I was once in a profession where being unstoppable was part of the job description. Prior to becoming a journalist, I was a neonatal resuscitation nurse. I attended high-risk births where there could be complications—a premature delivery, multiple births (twins, triplets, or more!), respiratory distress—making a fragile newborn's entry into the world difficult and necessitating life-saving care. And if the baby arrived before the pediatric doctor on call got to the labor floor, I was often the first responder, providing oxygen, warmth, an IV, or other urgent care for the little one.

So whenever I was called to attend a high-risk birth, I became unstoppable in doing what I had to do to get there and to provide the immediate care needed until the newborn was safely in his or her mother's arms or in the neonatal intensive care unit.

Now, an unstoppable resuscitation nurse is different from someone committed to manifesting a lifelong dream, building an organization, or working to effect global change. But the same principles apply. Becoming unstoppable is more than just a decision—it's a way of being. It means leaving your comfort zone and making your vision—and those you are serving—more important than being "comfortable."

As a resuscitation nurse, I was forced to leave my comfort zone on a regular basis. I had to commit to my role of providing critical care, even when circumstances were beyond my control. In many cases, I had to "keep calm and carry on," knowing that support would ultimately arrive—maybe. I had to find creative solutions when problems arose, make the best possible use of available resources, and get used to being in the adrenaline-filled zone of the unknown.

In every case, I did my unstoppable best to be a force for good and live up to the mission of every medical professional—to provide the best possible care for the life with which I was entrusted and, above all, as those in the medical profession pledge, to "do no harm."

In this chapter, we'll explore being "unstoppable" in following your truth; achieving results through creativity, adaptability, and resourcefulness; and getting comfortable being *un*comfortable as you build momentum toward your vision. We'll also meet the woman who literally wrote the book on how to be unstoppable.

Committing to the Vision

"When you want something, all the universe conspires in helping you to achieve it," Paulo Coelho writes in *The Alchemist*. That said, the realization of any great dream or desire requires the commitment to follow it through to completion. Transformational author Cynthia Kersey believes, "The greatest natural resource in the world is not in the earth's waters or minerals, nor in the forests or grasslands. It is the spirit that resides in every unstoppable person." And it's that spirit of fierce determination to proceed without compromise that ultimately benefits us all.

CYNTHIA KERSEY is the chief humanitarian officer of the Unstoppable Foundation and best-selling author of two books, *Unstoppable* and *Unstoppable Women*. Her vision is to ensure that every child on the planet has access to the lifelong gift of education. Through the foundation's international programs, it has already built six primary schoolhouses and two secondary schools for girls in three African countries. Cynthia is also a speaker, entrepreneur, national columnist, team coach, and philanthropist. Her upcoming book, *Unstoppable Giving*, teaches people the power of building a life and business around generosity; it shows entrepreneurs how they can expand their business through a philosophy of contribution.

For more information, visit
www.unstoppablefoundation.org

Cynthia Kersey's own journey, from successful career woman in corporate America to philanthropist and founder of an international nonprofit organization, exemplifies what it means to be unstoppable. As the chief humanitarian officer of the aptly named Unstoppable Foundation, Cynthia has a vision that every child on the planet will have access to the lifelong gift of education.

Working in 14 communities in Africa, the Unstoppable Foundation has helped to fund over 70 schools in three countries: Kenya, Uganda, and Liberia. It has aided in providing education to more than 7,000 children a day, and it brings clean water, sanitation, health care, and training to almost 30,000 community members.

It all started with Cynthia's desire to do something that was meaningful and "on purpose." Having worked at Sprint Communications for over ten years, Cynthia had moved up through the ranks to become a national account manager, handling a multimillion-dollar account. She had made it to the top in her career.

The problem was that Cynthia wasn't passionate about what she was doing. Reflecting on her life and career, she realized she felt most inspired when she was encouraging other people. And what did she herself find most encouraging? The stories of people who were *unstoppable*: People who had a dream, vision, or goal and, despite all the things working against them, had the courage to say, *This is important, and I'm not going to let anything stop me.*

So, in 1996, Cynthia downsized her life, cashed in her entire life savings, and wrote her first book, *Unstoppable*. She was living on purpose, and life was good. Then, a year and a half after her book came out, everything changed. Cynthia's 20-year marriage ended, and her life was now at a turning point. Devastated by her divorce, she called her mentor, Millard Fuller, founder of Habitat for Humanity. Fuller gave her this advice: "When you have a great pain in your life, you need a greater purpose." But even though Cynthia had quit her job and put everything on the line to fulfill her purpose and write a book, it wasn't bigger than her pain.

Fuller had another idea. He suggested that Cynthia build a house with Habitat for Humanity. He had just returned from Nepal and told her about how beautiful but impoverished the people there were. Cynthia thought about it, asking herself how many houses she would need to build to make her pain seem less important than what she could do for others. The number that finally got her inspired was one hundred!

At the time, it cost two thousand dollars to build a Habitat for Humanity house, so that meant it would take two hundred thousand dollars to fulfill this new purpose—a fair chunk of change for someone who had never raised any money in her life. She also had never been to Nepal, didn't have a big network of contacts, and didn't have a lot of resources.

But what she did have was commitment, focus, and an unstoppable spirit. In the year following her divorce, a time of healing and grieving, she thought about families who didn't even have a simple, decent place to live—and what she could do about it. *Wow, this feels inspiring to me,* she thought.

She decided to "get over herself" and move forward. That year, through speaking engagements, she raised two hundred thousand dollars and took a group of 18 donors to Nepal to meet the people and see what Habitat was doing there. The next holiday season, she personally worked on the first three of the one hundred homes that were subsequently built. That experience—a pivotal event—was the impetus for her future philanthropic work. It allowed Cynthia to truly experience the power of giving and its capacity to transform lives—both the giver's and the receiver's.

Paying Attention to Unexpected Opportunities

In 2008, Cynthia reached another turning point when she was invited to go to a conference in rural Africa. Although the timing wasn't convenient and she had to reschedule her prior commitments, she thought, *I need to do this.* She booked a last-minute trip to Nairobi, flew to East Africa, and was met by 40 other women from North America. They got on a bus with no air conditioning and rode for two days to what seemed like the middle of nowhere.

Before reaching her destination, Cynthia made a quiet plea to God: *Please help me get over my little self, so I don't miss why I'm here.*

When she and the others arrived, they were greeted by four hundred women from the heart of Kenya, many from rural communities who had walked for days to be with the North American women and share their stories.

The African women were looking for solutions, not handouts. Cynthia fell in love with them and promised she would do something to help them. The number one thing they wanted to know was how to get their kids an education. They knew that without education, there was no hope of stopping the cycle of poverty.

Creativity loves a good challenge. When we face obstacles in life, we are often forced to reconsider old ideas and look for new ways to get what we want. Success in reaching our goals and completing our projects often follows a series of smart choices based on creative thinking.

When Cynthia returned home, she had no idea how she was going to raise money to help the women she had met in Africa. That is, until she attended a friend's son's bar mitzvah. Instead of getting gifts, he asked people to donate to build a school. As he was talking about the school, Cynthia sat up and thought, *That's what I want to do for my birthday.* Her 50th birthday was coming up, and until that moment, she had not been looking forward to celebrating it. But she *was* excited about having a fundraiser—a birthday party that would make a difference. She charged people $100 and hired somebody to help her put the party together. That night, she raised $80,000!

It was the single most joyful day of Cynthia's life. *Wow,* she thought, *if I could do that in one night, what could I do if I actually focused on it and put a little energy into it?* The result was the Unstoppable Foundation, which she created in 2008, and which hosts annual galas and raises hundreds of thousands of dollars for its programs in Africa.

In 2011, Cynthia reached another crossroads. Alongside her foundation work, she had been coaching and speaking. She now felt that she was "done" running this business—she had no desire to do another coaching program, send another e-mail blast, or continue other aspects of the operation that were no longer fulfilling. She wanted to run the Unstoppable Foundation full-time. But she didn't know exactly how she was going to do it.

Again, inspiration, creativity, and help came calling.

Reaching out for Support

Cynthia talked to two friends, and they came up with a strategy to call three people a day and request their support. Cynthia named the campaign "Give a Little, Get a Lot." She phoned three people a day and asked them to donate either a product or money. She had wanted to do this full-time for many years. Once she committed, everything lined up to support her. People donated money. Her friends and colleagues Nick and Alice Ortner not only donated $50,000 but also offered to manage the entire campaign for free.

Today, completely inspired, Cynthia runs the Unstoppable Foundation, as well as a program called Unstoppable Giving, and is grateful for her life's work. "Wow, what a way to live," she says. "My life gets to be about inspiring people to give. That's the greatest blessing that anybody can experience."

People sometimes ask Cynthia why she chose to focus her work in Africa when women and children in North America are also in dire need. She says she committed to going where the need was greatest, after discovering that 57 million children in Africa don't have access to a primary education. And 43 percent of those children—almost half of them—live in Sub-Saharan Africa, where the Unstoppable Foundation focuses.

According to the United Nations, education has a greater impact than any form of aid. When Cynthia heard this, she decided to dedicate herself to supporting education. "For every year a child goes to school, especially a girl, HIV rates go down, income potentials and rates of employment increase, girls get married later, early pregnancy rates decline, and nutrition and health are elevated in the entire family."

Staying True to Your Calling

There's another reason Cynthia focuses her work in Africa. "You have to stay true to your calling," she says. She is called to communities that not only lack schools but also do not have basic services, such as clean water and simple health care. Without access to clean water, girls and moms are fetching contaminated water three or four times a day. And no health services are available when a woman goes into labor or if a child gets malaria. Education becomes secondary if a family cannot attain clean water, food, and basic health care—sick children do not go to school, and poor families cannot afford to send them.

Being unstoppable is not always easy. At a very fundamental level, it's about having a dream, goal, or purpose and not letting circumstances or, more importantly, yourself, stop you from really taking a stand. Cynthia didn't always feel comfortable asking people for money, but at each level of putting herself "out there," she got used to feeling uncomfortable.

Inspired to champion education for all children, starting with those in Africa, Cynthia Kersey has stayed connected to what she is doing and why, without bowing to limitations or obstacles. Her success and momentum are fueled by her "unstoppable" action, creativity, hard work, and genuine belief in the power of giving. These qualities have propelled her dream forward and continue to expand her vision—in Africa and beyond.

Lessons to Take with You

Being unstoppable can be uncomfortable, as it often requires you to stretch beyond your limits, skills, and beliefs. However, being committed to your purpose and staying true to your calling will give you the will, tenacity, and courage to keep going despite difficult circumstances or obstacles. Those with an unstoppable spirit proceed with focused determination and without compromise.

Questions for Contemplation

1. Are you willing to not allow obstacles or circumstances to stop you? Being unstoppable is more than a decision; it's a way of being.

2. Are there opportunities that you have ignored? How can you make sure to catch the next one?

3. How committed are you to your dream or vision?

4. How can you align your true calling with your organization, business, or the world you envision?

ACTION
AGAINST ALL REASON

*"The reasonable man adapts himself to the world; the
unreasonable one persists in trying to adapt the world to himself.
Therefore all progress depends on the unreasonable man."*

~ George Bernard Shaw ~

Sometimes it pays to be unreasonable—not just to "think outside the box" but to conceive a *new* box! That's where real genius thrives. Powerful creators and agents of change understand this. In fact, while some of their ideas may be considered unreasonable, others may be deemed just plain crazy.

I've done a few things in my life that some have considered crazy while others have seen as courageous: relocating to Los Angeles on a whim; moving to the south of France for a year of living outrageously; and, on another "hunch," purchasing a four-thousand-square-foot house on a sprawling riverfront property, when I was single and without a full-time job. Unreasonable, perhaps. Irrational, maybe. Life-changing, absolutely. In every case, when I had the will and persistence to take action, everything and everyone aligned to bring my vision to fruition.

Regarding the riverfront property, my intention was to turn this magnificent space into a place of healing, light, and possibility—where guests would feel better when they left than when they had arrived. Based on what visitors told me, my intention was realized. The house, with cedar shakes and soaring elevations (45 feet at its peak), had a magnetism that attracted the extraordinary: I hosted eight Tibetan monks for dinner and a sacred ceremony; held fundraisers for artists and musicians; celebrated milestone birthdays and events; and put together legendary parties for 120 to 150 people—friends, acquaintances, and complete strangers—who mingled and met seamlessly. People still rave about those gatherings. And while I may not have solved the world's problems there, I certainly had deep conversations about them.

This fantastic riverside dwelling in a parklike setting became a kind of transformative space—a wellspring of creativity, inspiration, and peace. The house was also a venue where I raised money for causes I cared about. And as a journalist, I wrote some of my best stories there. It was the most unreasonable—and delightful—purchase I ever made. Today that living work of art, which I restored, is on a Winnipeg Art Gallery tour of the city's most architecturally notable homes.

The power of the unreasonable and the ingenuity of the unconventional cannot be underestimated. As a television commercial for Apple said about misfits and rebels, the ones who see things differently: "They push the human race forward, and while some may see them as the crazy ones, we see genius, because the people who are crazy enough to think they can change the world are the ones who do."

The mind-sets, strategies, and practices of "unreasonable" visionaries set them apart, and the conditions they create allow high-level creativity to flourish. Indeed, those with rebellious ways who think differently are solving some of the world's most pressing problems. One captivating entrepreneur who certainly fits into the "rebel" category is Daniel Epstein. Daniel is founder of the Unreasonable Institute and the Unreasonable Group, organizations that support entrepreneurs who tackle major social and environmental challenges around the globe.

Being an Entrepreneur

When it comes to creating, Daniel Epstein has a heavy bias toward action—both in business and in his lifestyle. By the time Daniel earned a BA in philosophy, he had started three ventures in Boulder, Colorado. He cofounded two companies, one focused on making education more affordable and another dedicated to conservation and development through ecotourism. In 2012, Daniel was recognized by *Inc.* magazine as one of the "30 Coolest Entrepreneurs Under 30" and by *Forbes* as one of the top 30 most impactful entrepreneurs of the year.

DANIEL EPSTEIN founded the Unreasonable Institute in 2009 with a team of people who shared his healthy disregard for the impossible. This organization provides mentorship, funding, and a global network to entrepreneurs whose ventures have the potential to improve the lives of large numbers of people. Daniel has also established the Unreasonable Group, whose vision is to create a portfolio of companies that will put a dent in the major social and environmental challenges of this century. Daniel is cofounder of two companies: Tuition Specialists, focused on making education more affordable; and Unreasonable Adventures, dedicated to ecotourism. He has been recognized for his entrepreneurship by Forbes and Inc. magazines.

For more information, visit *www.unreasonablegroup.com*

In the summer of 2008, Daniel directed his entrepreneurial energy to cofound and lead a five-week institute that brought 17 young, aspiring social entrepreneurs from 14 different countries together in Boulder to understand and address key global issues. This event was the forerunner of the Unreasonable Institute, an organization that today brings together about 25 entrepreneurs from 20 countries and puts them under the same roof for six weeks a year in an environment where ideas, innovation, and investors meet head-on and thrive.

The environment at the Unreasonable Institute is as undisciplined and creatively charged as one might expect with a group of obsessive entrepreneurs who don't fit in anywhere else but who are dying to see their visions—and their companies—succeed. These young visionaries believe that only action can validate theoretical knowledge. And life is too short *not* to be unreasonable.

With the conviction that entrepreneurship is the answer to nearly all the issues we face today, Daniel has dedicated his life to supporting businesses that are truly changing the planet. He can't understand the notion of stumbling your way through a problem or attempting to solve tough challenges by talking—he prefers action!

There's a big difference between theory and practice. The only way to truly test or improve something is to put it into practice. In the day-to-day work of innovation, it's action—even flawed action—that unlocks the creative forces that help reorganize, re-sequence, and restructure ideas.

Daniel has discovered that the best go-to-market strategy for solving a problem is, well, to go to market. That—and empathy—are the keys to finding solutions to the world's really tough challenges. You build empathy by prototyping and getting things to market—and receiving feedback from the marketplace. The action sequence looks something like this: prototype, go to market, listen to the market, adapt, prototype, and go to market again. Eventually, you'll arrive at an insight through experience, not through discussion.

Creating Success Through Failure

It has been said that success is going from failure to failure without losing enthusiasm. Part of being unreasonable is accepting failure as part of success. In challenging the status quo, you have to be willing to experiment—and sometimes fail—before a solution appears.

According to Daniel, the Unreasonable Institute would rather achieve 20 percent of the impossible than 100 percent of the possible, if the goal is worthy enough. Failing 80 percent of the time is allowed, because succeeding 20 percent of the time is worth it when you're dealing with critical issues like extreme poverty, shelter, and access to clean drinking water. Success depends not only on the determination to attempt new things but also on the humility to admit that failure is possible.

The Unreasonable Institute creates the conditions in which ideas and people productively collide. Daniel calls these collisions and subsequent fruitful relationships "relational alchemy." The main job of the Unreasonable Institute is to act as convener, matching up the world's most promising entrepreneurs with mentors and investors who will help take ideas to the next level.

It sounds a bit like a dating service, but bold entrepreneurs meet the mentors and investors they need, in conditions where creativity and imagination flourish. Ultimately, the goal is to get the smartest people on earth to work on the hardest problems.

What happens within the Unreasonable Institute's programs almost feels like magic—but it's real. For example, one program is a company in India that offers the largest offline search capability in the world. With about 130 million active users, it's the brainchild of a 20-year-old entrepreneur who looked around India and realized that only 11 percent of the country had access to the Internet, while 88 percent had access to phones with SMS (a system for sending short text messages) but no Internet. So, he essentially created Google for

SMS. For example, you can text a number and say, "Driving directions from Mumbai to Chennai," and the system will send you step-by-step driving directions—for free.

Like its founder, the Unreasonable Institute believes desperately and obsessively in entrepreneurs. Most of the world sees issues, problems, and challenges; entrepreneurs see opportunities and solutions. At the Unreasonable Institute, all problems are not created equal—and these entrepreneurs want to work on the hardest ones. Moreover, they are willing to risk everything to find the solutions.

For Daniel, the key to success is achieving convergence between what makes you come alive, what you can live with, and what you can be best at in the world. His advice: "As much as possible, listen to your gut. Don't listen to the social constructions of what's appropriate because that's not the life you want to live. Follow what you believe in, and do it. It sounds cheesy, but it's that simple. It's just taking that posture, standing up a little bit differently, and saying: 'I'm going to do what I really believe in, and I'll find a way to make it work because the solution is not certain and it is not given to me.'"

We can lead lives in which the solutions to problems remain undiscovered, or we can create our own paths and our own visions—but doing so requires a different posture, an unreasonable posture.

The process of problem solving is completely different from creating, says Robert Fritz, author of *The Path of Least Resistance*. "When you are solving a problem, you are taking action to have something go away: *the problem*. When you are creating, you are taking action to have something come into being: *the creation*." Most people have been raised to focus on problem solving with little exposure to or practice in the creative process. Within the Unreasonable Institute, creativity and alternative ideas—however irrational or illogical—are the driving forces behind getting desired results and realizing visions. The "crazy ones" are leaders who are not afraid to be unreasonable, because lives may depend on it.

Lessons to Take with You

Unreasonable ways of thinking, beyond logic, can drive the creativity and alternative ideas necessary to solve big challenges. Also, in order to succeed, you must be willing to fail—often. Innovation requires action, and usually several adaptations, before a solution emerges. Action—even flawed action—unlocks creative forces. Ideas, inventions, and innovations must be put into practice in order to test their effectiveness.

Questions for Contemplation

1. Where in your life can you take inspired action?

2. In what areas can you embrace failure as part of success and still keep going?

3. Where can you find convergence between what makes you come alive, what you can live with, and what you're best at in the world?

4. Are you willing to be "unreasonable?" (Note: Lives may depend on it.)

FOCUS
CREATING THE REALITY YOU DESIRE

"The best way to predict the future is to design it."
—Buckminster Fuller

Visionary leaders achieve extraordinary things, not only because they allow themselves to imagine extraordinary possibilities but also because they consciously focus on the end result, or material object, they want to bring into the world. Albert Einstein said imagination is more important than knowledge. In the 1960s, it was President John F. Kennedy's ability to imagine, and then focus on, putting a man on the moon that fueled the American space program and led to Neil Armstrong's stepping out onto the lunar surface in 1969.

Focus can have a very personal impact. "Your focus creates your reality," as my friend and mentor William Whitecloud says in his book, *The Magician's Way*. Not long ago, I wanted to create the reality of living by the ocean; I was more than ready to leave the landlocked

Canadian prairies (and their arctic-like winters), where I was living at the time. Over the years, I'd lived in Australia, California, and the south of France, and even spent a few months testing the waters in Maui, but hadn't quite found the "right" seaside address.

So without getting caught up in the geographic location, I focused on the end result of a beautiful home near the ocean, in a mild climate, where I could live, work, and travel easily. Bingo. In a flash of genius, the idea came to me to move to the coast of my own country! I know, how obvious. But honestly, it was something my global soul—accustomed to traveling and living in other countries—had never considered until that point.

That was in April 2014. I spent that summer checking out places to live in Victoria, on Vancouver Island, and moved to this west coast city by October of the same year. My new reality includes residing in a neighborhood that looks like a botanical garden, in a charming midcentury-modern condo, about a five-minute walk from the water and not far from where the cruise ships come in. Apparently, I live on a destination island. Note to self: Focus creates reality.

As in the example about President Kennedy's ambitious goal to send an American to the moon, focus can be directed to the cosmos as well as to life on earth. Few things have more power to spark imagination and motivate the creation of big dreams than the exploration of space—truly the final frontier. And soon, space travel may not be limited to professional astronauts and the extremely wealthy who are able to buy a six-figure ticket to fly into a low orbit around Earth.

In this chapter, we'll meet a visionary leader who is truly shooting for the stars. Shubham Garg believes nothing is more powerful than an idea whose time has come, and he and his team of galactic explorers, including former astronauts, are focused on the idea of democratizing space travel—to send ordinary citizens from all over the world far above the planet!

Reaching for the Stars

To succeed beyond your wildest expectations, you have to begin with some wild expectations. Shubham Garg exemplifies the power of focus and what can happen when you tap into resources and develop the structure necessary to create the reality that was once an impossible dream. Shubham was 14 when he witnessed his first meteor shower over the night sky in India, a sight so magnificent it humbled him and made him acutely aware that "we are all traveling through space on . . . Spaceship Earth!"

Fascinated by space from that moment on, Shubham decided to become an actual rocket scientist. He spent the next decade pursuing multiple degrees from reputable schools, learning software development, and teaching students in the far reaches of India— all to further a continuing focus on the space industry. He even led a team to create India's first private high-altitude balloon mission. In addition, he organized a one-time event: India's first solar eclipse cruise, which took 900 people to the Maldives to view an eclipse from the best possible location. Shubham moved to the United States from India in

SHUBHAM GARG is chief visionary officer of the Star Harbor Space Training Academy, which he cofounded with entrepreneur Maraia Hoffman in 2013 to make space travel more available to private citizens. Fascinated by space from a young age, Shubham obtained a master's degree in astronautical engineering from the University of Southern California in 2012, specializing in interplanetary space navigation. In addition to founding the Star Harbor Space Training Academy, Shubham and Hoffman joined with other leaders in the aerospace industry, including former NASA astronauts, to create Spaceship Earth Grants (SEG), the world's first global, crowdfunded scholarship to send private citizens into space. In 2015, SEG partnered with another company and evolved to become Kruger Cowne's Rising Star Programme.

For more information, visit *www.krugercowne.com/risingstar*

2010 in still another step toward his dream. He attained his master's degree in astronautical engineering from the University of Southern California, specializing in interplanetary space navigation. When Shubham started thinking about what he wanted to do after he graduated from USC in 2012, he might have had this insightful saying in mind: "Dream no small dreams for they have no power to move the hearts of men."

Then, what became a global incident in December 2012, the brutal gang rape and fatal assault of a young woman on a bus in Delhi, left him in a state of outrage, shame, and disappointment. Beyond the rape incident, he knew that people in India were suffering in so many other ways: extreme poverty, malnutrition, lack of clean water, and more. In that moment, he decided to use his passion for space to do something that would not only help his homeland but also impact the world. His wild expectations now had a social focus: He wanted to use his scientific knowledge, space industry experience, and genius not only to move hearts but also to change minds, organizations, and global consciousness. Shubham wanted to start something that would create global awareness of the suffering in India and make people present to the human condition that exists everywhere on the planet—to remind people that we are all connected on "this tiny piece of rock called Earth."

But how?

Enter Maraia Hoffman, an astrophysicist and entrepreneur whom the young scientist met in early 2013. Maraia shared Shubham's desire to have a positive impact on the planet, and she was an advocate for the private space industry. Together, they brainstormed an idea to make the experience of space travel more available to, and more affordable for, private citizens. Until now, the two existing options for space travel—to pay about $250,000 to a private spaceflight provider or to be selected by a government space agency as an astronaut—have been obviously restrictive.

When they met, Maraia said to Shubham, "Put on your seatbelt. We are going to rock the world." In July 2013, they cofounded the Star Harbor Space Training Academy, with the vision to provide the transformational experience of seeing Earth from space to as many people as possible. The academy, a fully immersive spaceflight training facility, plans to open its doors to the public in 2019. At the time of this writing, the academy's executive team is finalizing a location in California or Colorado and looking for investors to get building underway.

The academy's goals are twofold: (1) to prepare people for actual spaceflight and (2) to give people who might never go into space but have dreamed of being an astronaut a place where they can train like one. The facility will offer training to prepare participants both physically and mentally to best manage their experience in space— everything from dealing with weightlessness to handling technology, communication, and daily activities. Different levels of training will be provided, with costs ranging from about $5,000 to $35,000.

Venturing into the Unknown

As Shubham and Maraia expanded on the idea of sending people into space, other leaders in the aerospace industry began to join their team, including former NASA astronauts Leland Melvin and Ron Garan. To forward the common goal of democratizing space, the group developed a proposal for a crowdfunded grant program: Spaceship Earth Grants (SEG). Joining the SEG council were Bill Nye, "the Science Guy," CEO of The Planetary Society; Alan Ladwig, former administrator and director of special projects at NASA; and some educators, authors, artists, and people in the media who shared a passion for space and making space travel accessible to all people. The plan was to sponsor an international spaceflight contest that would award the person with the "right stuff" an opportunity to travel into space for free.

Then, in 2015, Shubham's dream took still another turn, enabling a quicker startup. Under the initiative of Ron Garan, SEG decided to partner with the talent agency Kruger Cowne; the spaceship grants evolved to become Kruger Cowne's Rising Star Programme, in which one winner was chosen for a suborbital flight 100 kilometers (62 miles) in space. The Rising Star contest received applications from 90 countries and shortlisted the entries to 30 inspiring young leaders. Three finalists were chosen to present their case for going into space before a panel of high-profile judges at the One Young World Summit in Bangkok in November 2015.

The first winner of the contest, and "Rising Star," is Hussain Manawer, an online media entrepreneur, humanitarian, and former Olympic torchbearer in his 20s from the United Kingdom, who has raised thousands of dollars for national and international charities. He will take flight in 2018 aboard an XCOR Aerospace spacecraft, but the larger goal of the program is that he will share his experience and its impact with as many others as possible.

Shubham's vision is about creating change in the space travelers, their communities, and the world when they come back. When former NASA space shuttle astronaut Leland Melvin went into space, he said that it fundamentally changed his life, and he wanted others to have the same experience. He believed that the transformational experience of seeing Earth from space and viewing the planet from a much higher—indeed, global—perspective could influence how we think, act, and respond to life on earth.

It's called the "overview effect," says Shubham. "Seeing Earth from space makes you realize we're all living on this tiny piece of rock called Earth, and all the problems we have are man-made, yet they can be resolved." The overview effect often creates a cognitive shift in the person in space: Most astronauts come back wanting to do something to improve the quality of life on the planet. This shift—perceiving the planet as a unified whole rather than separate countries, continents, and borders—is part of the positive, global impact Shubham and his colleagues hope to achieve by awarding space travel to individuals.

But that's not all. Shubham realized that about 560 people out of 7 billion had gone to space, and most of those able to look down on Earth from space had been military pilots, astronauts, or scientists. What if artists, writers, and musicians could go up into space, experience the overview effect, and share their transformation through their creations? They could present an entirely different perspective.

For Shubham, it's not just about sending people into space but using space travel to raise global consciousness. A related goal is to use the experience of space travel to work toward projects that will transform some of the biggest issues here on our planetary home, such as hunger, poverty, and lack of clean water—not just in India, but all over the world. As part of his greater vision, in the long term, Shubham also wants to bring private space-related industries to India.

Although Shubham has not yet traveled into space, he'd like to—but he'll wait his turn. At 30, this young visionary says creating the spaceflight academy is far more exciting than a "real job," and changing the planet is a lot more fun! He says, "I was born in a reality I did not choose, but I choose to live in a reality that I create. That's why today we have a program sending 'Rising Stars' to space."

Lessons to Take with You

Focus creates reality. What you place your conscious attention on is what will manifest in your life. Our reality, including our experiences and perceptions, is created by what we focus on. Powerful creators always begin with the end in mind—focusing on the end result without knowing exactly how it will be accomplished. They focus on the "what" and let the "how" unfold by being open to possibilities not yet known.

Also, a new perspective can change perception. For example, viewing Earth from space and seeing it as a unified whole rather than separate countries or continents may shift how we treat our global home.

Questions for Contemplation

1. Are your dreams big enough? The possibilities for change are limited only by your imagination.

2. Are you willing to venture into the unknown and build something new, without "knowing what you don't know" before you begin?

3. Do you know like-minded people, with similar values and goals, whose expertise and resources could expand your vision—from global to beyond?

4. Consider the power of the overview effect. What new perspective could help you look at something differently?

WILL

BRINGING YOUR VISION TO LIFE

*"A hero is someone who has given his or her life
to something bigger than oneself."*

~ Joseph Campbell ~

In the classic hero's journey, the hero is called to leave the ordinary world and go on a quest. He or she then faces and overcomes some extraordinary struggle or trauma, gaining a treasure (such as wisdom). Finally, the hero returns home with the treasure, which may now be used to serve the community, tribe, or world at large. In the context of contemporary visionaries, as mythologist and author Joseph Campbell suggested in the opening quote, heroes are those who give their lives to a mission or some great purpose.

Early in my quest to give my life to something bigger, I healed people—in some cases, saving their lives—as a nurse. Later, I sought to be a force for good through the stories I wrote and published. Now I plan to write about as well as teach others how to create the highest expressions of their visions. Ultimately, my own evolution, like all hero's journeys, will require will and the choice to "go for it," no matter what.

Carl Jung said, "People will do anything, no matter how absurd, in order to avoid facing their own souls." I believe my hero's journey is to be an example of facing—and embracing—your soul's expression to the point that even being hit by a car (a few times) won't defeat you. And interacting with your soul is not only empowering, it can be deep fun . . . indeed, deep play. As Jung also said, "The creative mind plays with objects it loves." Really, is there any better reason to be on the planet?

All of the heroes featured in this book have certainly dedicated their lives to something bigger than themselves. They have engaged in what I call "deep play"—even if it involved *serious* problems and situations. While they genuinely love what they do, they also have the will and fierce determination to stick with their vision until it becomes reality. Nothing changes in life without the willingness to choose and commit to whatever it is you truly want. Will keeps your dreams alive. As William Whitecloud says in *The Magician's Way*, "The more meaningful a creation is to your heart, the more commitment it takes to stay with it. . . . It's all too easy to give away the dream of your heart and buy into the reality of your mind or, even worse, other people's minds."

In this chapter, we'll meet someone with a strong will, someone whose vision has, in his own words, "become a life commitment." He's a Haitian-born teacher, author, and poet now living in Canada, whose mission to bring change to his homeland was so strong that not even a catastrophic earthquake could shake him from his goals.

Educating to Transform

Sometimes a single idea can transform a million realities. That's the story of Dr. Bathélemy Bolivar. After hearing that an earthquake in January 2010 decimated much of his homeland, Haiti, he was determined to address the education gap in that country—which had been exacerbated by the earthquake.

BATHÉLEMY BOLIVAR is a Haitian-born teacher, essayist, and award-winning poet now living in Winnipeg, Canada. A passionate educator, he has a master of education degree and a PhD in mathematics and science education from the University of Manitoba, as well as a master of e-business from Université Laval. In 2011, Bathélemy established Haitian School without Borders (HSWB), an ambitious online education project to support reconstruction efforts in Haiti after the January 2010 earthquake devastated the country and many of its schools.

For more information, visit *www.haitianschoolwithoutborders.org*

After losing their schools, and in some cases their teachers, many young people were left without education after the quake. Bathélemy was already aware that Haiti had a kind of elitist educational system that did not give everybody access to quality schooling. There was a huge gap between the "haves" and the "have-nots," and after the earthquake, that gap was even wider.

Bathélemy's mission was born: to do whatever it took to provide free, quality education to anyone who wanted it, by developing educational programs online. And that's exactly what he did when he established the nonprofit organization Haitian School without Borders (École *haitienne sans Frontières*). A powerful combination of technology and innovation in educational instruction, this online program provides virtual classes for students and important resources for teachers. It was not intended to replace the Haitian school system—standard teaching practices and the local curriculum are maintained—but rather to enhance it.

The seed for Bathélemy's vision was planted through his own remarkable journey with education. When he was growing up in Haiti, Bathélemy was lucky enough to attend Catholic elementary and secondary schools, and later a Catholic university. So although he didn't come from a wealthy or privileged family, he was exposed to a high standard of education.

In 2002, Bathélemy came north to Winnipeg, Canada, to begin a career teaching science and technology in both English and French at the high school level; he has since gone on to teach at the University of Manitoba. His journey from Haiti to Canada was life-changing, and he wanted to share with other Haitians what had been possible for him. He believed with every fiber of his being that only quality education could make a difference in someone's life—"not merely education, but *quality* education," he stresses.

Bathélemy was shocked that 50 percent of the schools in Haiti closed after the 2010 earthquake. Most of these schools were concentrated in urban areas, and the rebuilding process was slow. On visits to Haiti even three years after the quake, he noted that a few schools still held classes in tents.

But brighter days were—and are—to come. Haitian School without Borders aims to put 30 to 40 classes online for the four years of high school that most students take. In the program's first phase, the organization implemented ten of these classes, with 30 modules for students, and added five more classes at the end of 2015.

Sustaining the Vision Through Faith

When a strong will conspires with deep conviction, obstacles and limits fall away to create a space where nothing seems impossible. Faith helps summon the courage, and will provides the stamina, to "keep calm and carry on" through whatever detours or roadblocks are thrown your way—whether it's a lack of funding, not enough time or resources to bring projects to fruition, or a necessary adjustment to the original vision because it's no longer feasible.

Despite all the problems with Haiti's post-earthquake infrastructure, Bathélemy's conviction to provide young Haitians with a decent education allowed him to adapt his vision. Originally, he had thought of going to Haiti and opening new schools. But once the earthquake hit, the need and mission became much more critical. Less than a year later, Haitian School without Borders was born. Funding was, and still is, one of HSWB's major obstacles. Bathélemy has created much of the program with his own money, supplemented by fundraising and private donations. He and teachers he continues to recruit have also volunteered their time to design a lot of the online content.

In later phases of the program, Bathélemy plans to increase awareness and garner support from students, teachers, and principals within Haiti and to collaborate with that country's Internet providers and information technology companies for technical support.

An earthquake may have shaken the conventional educational system, but through Haitian School without Borders, students need only Internet access to take classes; their education can continue even without a physical structure to go to!

Bathélemy's vision for Haitian School without Borders was to create something authentic, the kind of education that can promote change and really transform the country. And it does! Organized in a modern teaching style, and incorporating Haitian culture into the materials, the online program is interactive, using the best online technologies available, so any student with access to a mobile phone, tablet, or personal computer can have access to education.

Bathélemy tells the story of one student in his last year of high school who was unable to attend all of his classes. However, with access to HSWB's biology and English classes online, he followed the curriculum and passed his exams. In another scenario, a Haitian school had difficulty keeping its social studies teacher, who was sick and often absent. Even without their teacher, students continued their learning online through HSWB's social studies classes and passed their national exams.

Bringing any great vision into physical reality takes passion, will, and determination. Will assigns the power in your subconscious and lets it know you're serious about your dream. Bathélemy's unwavering belief that Haitian School without Borders could be a massive tool for change fueled his efforts and endurance until he was able to bring back the "treasure" to his community. His long hours of work to make affordable education available to students who have lost their schools and so much more will indeed serve to transform lives. That and his deeply held vision that *everybody*—with or without money—deserves a quality education, even if they don't have a physical school or stable ground beneath their feet.

Lessons to Take with You

To achieve any vision or dream, you must first believe—on a subconscious level—that it's possible. While faith and conviction in your beliefs will help you overcome obstacles, nothing changes in life without the willingness to take action and follow through. Your will assigns power in your consciousness. Creating change in the world is not so much a question of "Can I do it?" as "Will I do it?"

Enlisting the support of others, especially from within the community or industry you may be working in, will greatly accelerate bringing your vision to fruition.

Questions for Contemplation

1. Do you genuinely believe in your vision?

2. Do you have the will to persevere through sacrifices and challenges until change happens?

3. How might you enlist the support of others to help sustain your vision?

4. How might you work with leaders or other stakeholders to create change from *within* the community?

CONCLUSION
WHY FOLLOW YOUR TRUTH?

"It's not what the vision is, it's what the vision does."
~ Peter M. Senge ~

I wrote this book to follow my own heart and share a few stories—both mine and other people's—as reflections on the treasure of the hero's journey—a journey that can be daunting, exhausting, and, at times, seemingly futile. Yet we soldier on to bring our vision into the world and occasionally achieve the so-called "impossible."

I believe when we live from a place of truth and authentic power—from the higher consciousness that some call the place of genius—we can focus on *creating* what we want in the world rather than *reacting* to what we don't want.

In the end, I agree with Robert Fritz: "When people make a fundamental choice to be true to what is highest in them, or when they make a choice to fulfill a purpose in their life, they can easily accomplish many changes that seemed impossible or improbable in the past.... When people are united with their real power—the power to create what they want to create—they always choose what is highest in humanity...challenges worthy of the human spirit." Therefore, creating what we love—the true expression of our soul's nature, deep play, or deep truth—is what will change the world. All of the leaders featured in this book certainly have altruistic tendencies; however, the primary motivation for their work started with answering the call of their soul—their unstoppable vision or great dream.

"The truth is not discretionary," says William Whitecloud. In other words, our specific dreams come to us for a reason: because *we* have the ability, desire, and capacity to achieve them, even if we need additional resources or training to do so. Our job is to follow our truth until the final results are in. The reason most people do not become true creative forces in their lives or experience deep transformation is because they compromise, adjust, or give up on their dream before it's realized. To reiterate the earlier quote from Robert Fritz: "The human spirit will not invest itself in a compromise." He also noted: "After the direct experience of creating what they have chosen, these people know that what they want is not arbitrary."

There are some magnificent examples of doggedly pursuing what one has been called to create, knowing that this calling is not arbitrary, in a short film series that director Errol Morris produced for the *New York Times*. It features notable peacemakers. One is Leymah Gbowee, a young Liberian woman who was called in a dream to "wake up and gather the women of the churches to pray for peace." This was at the time of Liberia's blood-soaked civil war and extreme violence under the brutal dictatorship of President Charles G. Taylor.

Although the dream seemed to be asking the impossible, Leymah believed "the dream bearer is the dream carrier," as she says in the film, and because the dream had come to her, it was for her to carry it out. And she did. An unwed mother with few resources, she united the women in her country in nonviolent protests for peace, met face-to-face-with Charles Taylor, rallied thousands of women to attend peace talks in Ghana, and, through her activism, helped force Taylor out of power. In 2011, Leymah received the Nobel Peace Prize.

In the film series, Morris also interviews Sir Bob Geldof, the Irish former rock star and honorary knight, about the "best day of [his] life." That day was July 13, 1985, when Geldof channeled the power of music and his rock-star connections to raise money to combat famine in Africa—a cause he was drawn to after seeing a short, dramatic news piece on television. Geldof and his high-profile friends performed at Wembley Stadium, in London, before 160,000 people in the now legendary Live Aid concert that raised about $140 million.

"The world is not immutable," Geldof says in the film. "You can change things, you really can." Today he still meets with political and world leaders to continue his humanitarian efforts.

Now these people may seem like the ultimate overachievers in turning their visions into reality but they simply embodied the same passion, will, and possibility that exist within all of us. As my favorite rocket scientist and the cofounder of Star Harbor Space Training Academy, Shubham Garg, reminds us: "We can choose to live in a reality that we create."

When we find something that inspires our soul, whether it's sending people into space, teaching meditation and mindfulness to schoolchildren, empowering women and girls in Uganda, or any other great creative endeavor, we see what is possible when the human heart and spirit conspire.

And there are a few more good reasons to create or do something that matters to you. Recent studies in neuroscience show that our brains, not just our hearts, are hardwired for giving. Being generous not only activates the pleasure centers in our brains, making us feel good, but it's also scientifically proven to improve our health, longevity, and overall happiness.

Dr. Stephen Post and Jill Neimark, authors of *Why Good Things Happen to Good People*, say giving to others improves your physical and mental health. "Give and you will be healthier. Give, and you will even live longer," they write.

Dr. Post runs The Institute for Research on Unlimited Love (IRUL), dedicated to exploring the power of giving, which has funded over 50 studies at 44 major universities. He has found that "giving will protect you your whole life long." In fact, research at his institute shows that giving reduces mortality, decreases depression, and promotes well-being. In what he calls "the science of love," studies have shown that giving protects overall health twice as much as aspirin protects against heart disease. "Giving is the most potent force on the planet," writes Dr. Post, and his vast research at IRUL suggests that doing good is good for us.

Unfortunately, most people do not spend their lives doing what they love, because deep down they don't believe they have the power to create what they desire. For many, life is about doing what they have to do, which may feed the human body but not the human spirit.

Our desire to create is one of our deepest human drives; and in addition to creating, many of us want to contribute, to give to something bigger than ourselves and have a significant impact in shaping the world. When you learn to create the "impossible" and tap into the power to manifest your own visions great and small, it serves your heart, happiness, and soul—and sometimes the planet.

As the primary creative force in your own universe, you can choose any end result. Therefore, following your truth can take many forms. Perhaps Rumi said it best: "Let the beauty we love be what we do. There are hundreds of ways to kneel and kiss the ground."

REFERENCES

Fritz, Robert. *The Path of Least Resistance.* Revised and expanded edition, New York: Fawcett Books, 1989. Originally published by Stillpoint Publishing, 1984.

Gilbert, Elizabeth. *Big Magic.* New York: Riverhead Books, 2015.

Osbon, Diane K. *A Joseph Campbell Companion.* Selected and Edited by Diane K. Osbon. Copyright 1991 by The Joseph Campbell Foundation. New York: HarperCollins Publishers.

Post, Stephen, Ph.D., and Neimark, Jill. *Why Good Things Happen to Good People.* New York: Broadway Books, 2007.

Tolle, Eckhart. *The Power of Now.* Novato, California: New World Library, 1999. Originally published in Canada by Namaste Publishing Inc., 1997.

Whitecloud, William. *The Magician's Way.* Novato, California: New World Library, 2009. Originally published in Australia, 2004.

ACKNOWLEDGMENTS

With deep appreciation and gratitude, I thank all the visionary people who granted interviews and graciously agreed to be part of this book. Thank you for your incredible stories, your shared wisdom and practices, and the great work you do in the world. You are way-showers for a kinder, richer, and more conscious planet.

I also offer great appreciation and gratitude to my many mentors who assisted in the development of this book and getting it out into the world, including Chris Attwood, Janet Bray Attwood, Marci Shimoff, and Geoff Affleck, as well as Charmaine Hammond, for your expertise, guidance, and unending support in all things book- (and marketing-) related. Special thanks to Marci Shimoff, my favorite happiness expert, who wrote the foreword. And straight-from-my-heart thanks to William Whitecloud, author of *The Magician's Way*, and creator of the "Meet Your Writer's Genius" training (and other programs at Natural Success International), who inspired and guided me to create a book that is a true expression of my soul. You are all role models of possibility and visionaries in your own right. I appreciate and honor you for all that you contribute to improving the lives of others and the world at large.

A huge thank you to my editor in chief, Brookes Nohlgren, and her superb team, who helped me bring my soul to the page and made this book better with their insights, clarity, and editing magic.

Sincere thanks to Vern and Joni at Blue Harvest Creative/BHC Press who handled all aspects of this book's design and publication.

Heartfelt thanks for the support of my many writer friends and colleagues, including members of the Evolutionary Business Council, especially its founder, Teresa de Grosbois, as well as my fellow "enlightened bestseller" authors Ellen Rogin, Dr. Shannon South,

Mary E. Knight, and so many others, who shared their stories and support in the early stages of this book.

Last, from the bottom of my heart, deep gratitude to my family, especially my sister Elaine Froese and brother Allan Edie, two of my biggest supporters and raving fans. And to my close friends, loved ones who've gone before me, and forces both seen and unseen, for their love, guidance, and unwavering belief in creating the "impossible." Thanks for the magic.

ABOUT THE AUTHOR

Barbara Edie believes a good story has the power to change lives. She's the author of *Sparking Change Around the Globe: 5 Ways to Make Your Difference in the World*, an Amazon bestseller, and the co-author of another bestseller, the *Manitoba Book of Everything*.

A writer and editor with a master of arts in journalism, she loves to share a great story—the wilder, the better—and is also an engaging speaker. Her storytelling and writing has been described as "inspiring, compelling, soul-shaking ... and highly entertaining." Pulitzer Prize-winning author Carol Shields, one of Barbara's former teachers, said she wrote "with wit and authority." Today, Barbara's just happy to keep her wits about her as she travels the globe to meet and tell stories of people "creating the impossible" and living soul-inspired lives way outside their comfort zone.

Barbara currently lives in Victoria, on Canada's glorious west coast.

Learn more about her writing and adventures at:
www.barbaraedie.com

CPSIA information can be obtained
at www.ICGtesting.com
Printed in the USA
LVOW03s0102030218
565159LV00001B/5/P

9 781946 006196